Time-Use Measurement and Research

Report of a Workshop

Committee on National Statistics

Michele Ver Ploeg, Joseph Altonji, Norman Bradburn, Julie DaVanzo, William Nordhaus, and Francisco Samaniego, *Editors*

Commission on Behavioral and Social Sciences and Education

National Research Council

NATIONAL ACADEMY PRESS
Washington, D.C.

NOTICE: The project that is the subject of this report was approved by the Governing Board of the National Research Council, whose members are drawn from the councils of the National Academy of Sciences, the National Academy of Engineering, and the Institute of Medicine. The members of the committee responsible for the report were chosen for their special competences and with regard for appropriate balance.

The project that is the subject of this report is supported by Contract SES-9709489 between the National Academy of Sciences and the U.S. Department of Labor and the National Institute of Aging. Support of the work of the Committee on National Statistics is provided by a consortium of federal agencies through a grant from the National Science Foundation (Number SBR-9709489). Any opinions, findings, conclusions, or recommendations expressed in this publication are those of the author(s) and do not necessarily reflect the view of the organizations or agencies that provided support for this project.

International Standard Book Number 0-309-07092-9

Additional copies of this report are available from National Academy Press, 2101 Constitution Avenue, N.W., Box 285, Washington, D.C. 20055. Call (800) 624-6242 or (202) 334-3313 (in the Washington metropolitan area). This report is also available on line at http://www.nap.edu

Printed in the United States of America

Suggested citation: National Research Council (2000) *Time-Use Measurement and Research: Report of a Workshop.* Committee on National Statistics. Michele Ver Ploeg, Joseph Altonji, Norman Bradburn, Julie DaVanzo, William Nordhaus, and Francisco Samaniego, Editors. Commission on Behavioral and Social Sciences and Education. Washington, DC: National Academy Press.

THE NATIONAL ACADEMIES

National Academy of Sciences
National Academy of Engineering
Institute of Medicine
National Research Council

The **National Academy of Sciences** is a private, nonprofit, self-perpetuating society of distinguished scholars engaged in scientific and engineering research, dedicated to the furtherance of science and technology and to their use for the general welfare. Upon the authority of the charter granted to it by the Congress in 1863, the Academy has a mandate that requires it to advise the federal government on scientific and technical matters. Dr. Bruce M. Alberts is president of the National Academy of Sciences.

The **National Academy of Engineering** was established in 1964, under the charter of the National Academy of Sciences, as a parallel organization of outstanding engineers. It is autonomous in its administration and in the selection of its members, sharing with the National Academy of Sciences the responsibility for advising the federal government. The National Academy of Engineering also sponsors engineering programs aimed at meeting national needs, encourages education and research, and recognizes the superior achievements of engineers. Dr. William A. Wulf is president of the National Academy of Engineering.

The **Institute of Medicine** was established in 1970 by the National Academy of Sciences to secure the services of eminent members of appropriate professions in the examination of policy matters pertaining to the health of the public. The Institute acts under the responsibility given to the National Academy of Sciences by its congressional charter to be an adviser to the federal government and, upon its own initiative, to identify issues of medical care, research, and education. Dr. Kenneth I. Shine is president of the Institute of Medicine.

The **National Research Council** was organized by the National Academy of Sciences in 1916 to associate the broad community of science and technology with the Academy's purposes of furthering knowledge and advising the federal government. Functioning in accordance with general policies determined by the Academy, the Council has become the principal operating agency of both the National Academy of Sciences and the National Academy of Engineering in providing services to the government, the public, and the scientific and engineering communities. The Council is administered jointly by both Academies and the Institute of Medicine. Dr. Bruce M. Alberts and Dr. William A. Wulf are chairman and vice chairman, respectively, of the National Research Council.

WORKSHOP PARTICIPANTS

Presenters and Discussants

Julie DaVanzo (*Chair*), RAND, Santa Monica, California*
Katharine Abraham, Bureau of Labor Statistics, U.S. Department of Labor
Joseph G. Altonji, Northwestern University*
Lorna Bailie, Statistics Canada, Ottawa
Suzanne Bianchi, University of Maryland
Michael Bittman, University of New South Wales, Australia
Rebecca M. Blank, U.S. Council of Economic Advisers
Norman Bradburn, National Opinion Research Center, University of
    Chicago
Jeanne Brooks-Gunn, Columbia University
Mihaly Csikszentmihalyi, University of Chicago
Nancy Folbre, University of Massachusetts, Amherst
Daniel Hamermesh, University of Texas, Austin
Anna Regula Herzog, University of Michigan
Sandra Hofferth, University of Michigan
Michael Horrigan, Bureau of Labor Statistics, U.S. Department of Labor
Dale Jorgenson, Harvard University
F. Thomas Juster, University of Michigan
J. Steven Landefeld, Bureau of Economic Analysis, U.S. Department of
    Commerce
Robert Michael, University of Chicago
William Nordhaus, Yale University*
Robert A. Pollak, Washington University
John P. Robinson, University of Maryland
John E. Rolph, University of Southern California*
Francisco J. Samaniego, University of California, Davis*
Jack E. Triplett, Brookings Institution, Washington, D.C.
Linda J. Waite, University of Chicago
Jiri Zuzanek, University of Waterloo, Canada

Other Participants

Donald M. Bay, National Agricultural Statistics Service, U.S. Department of
    Agriculture
Nancy Crowell, Board on Children, Youth, and Families, National Research
    Council

---

* Member, Committee on National Statistics

Cathryn Dippo, Bureau of Labor Statistics, U.S. Department of Labor
Vincent Fang, Bureau of Transportation Statistics, U.S. Department of
   Transportation
Barbara Fraumeni, Bureau of Economic Analysis, U.S. Department of
   Commerce
Jack Galvin, Bureau of Labor Statistics, U.S. Department of Labor
Caren Grown, The John D. and Catherine T. MacArthur Foundation,
   Chicago, Illinois
Nora Gordon, U.S. Council of Economic Advisers
Kenneth Hanson, Economic Research Service, U.S. Department of
   Agriculture
Andrew Harvey, Saint Mary's University, Canada
Diane Herz, Bureau of Labor Statistics, U.S. Department of Labor
Jennifer Holmstead, Economic Research Service, U.S. Department of
   Agriculture
Bradford R. Huther, Bureau of the Census, U.S. Department of Commerce
Mary Joyce, Bureau of Labor Statistics, U.S. Department of Labor
Ken Kaplan, Bureau of the Census, U.S. Department of Commerce
Kevin Kinsella, Committee on Population, National Research Council
Michele Kipke, Board on Children, Youth, and Families, National Research
   Council
Deborah Klein, Bureau of Labor Statistics, U.S. Department of Labor
Heather Koball, University of North Carolina
Edward Kokkelenberg, Binghamton University
Marilyn Manser, Bureau of Labor Statistics, U.S. Department of Labor
Stephanie McCulla, Bureau of Economic Analysis, U.S. Department of
   Commerce
William Mockovak, Bureau of Labor Statistics, U.S. Department of Labor
Daniel H. Newlon, U.S. National Science Foundation
Stanley Presser, University of Maryland
Cordelia Reimers, U.S. Council of Economic Advisers
Edwin Robison, Bureau of Labor Statistics, U.S. Department of Labor
Philip L. Rones, Bureau of Labor Statistics, U.S. Department of Labor
Kathleen Scholl, U.S. General Accounting Office
Ashish Sen, Bureau of Transportation Statistics, U.S. Department of
   Transportation
Stephanie Shipp, Bureau of the Census, U.S. Department of Commerce
James Spletzer, Bureau of Labor Statistics, U.S. Department of Labor
Jay Stewart, Bureau of Labor Statistics, U.S. Department of Labor
Linda Stinson, Bureau of Labor Statistics, U.S. Department of Labor
Miron L. Straf, Bureau of Transportation Statistics, U.S. Department of
   Transportation

Richard Suzman, National Institute on Aging
Barbara Torrey, Commission on Behavioral and Social Sciences and
    Education, National Research Council
Clyde Tucker, Bureau of Labor Statistics, U.S. Department of Labor
Stephen Vogel, Economic Research Service, U.S. Department of Agriculture

Staff

Michele Ver Ploeg, *Study Director*
Connie Citro, *Staff Officer*
Telissia Thompson, *Senior Project Assistant*

Acknowledgments

On behalf of the Committee on National Statistics (CNSTAT) and its subcommittee on the time-use workshop, I would like to thank the many people who generously contributed to the organization of the workshop and preparation of this summary. I first thank all the workshop participants, who presented interesting, high-quality papers, prepared formal discussions of the papers or who contributed to the exciting informal discussion at the workshop. I would like to recognize the contributions of my fellow subcommittee members, Joseph Altonji, Norman Bradburn, William Nordhaus, and Francisco Samaniego, for the time and terrific ideas they contributed to the planning of the workshop and to the preparation of this summary. Special thanks are extended as well to F. Thomas Juster and Robert A. Pollak for commenting on early versions of the workshop summary. Several staff members should be commended for their efforts towards the conduct of the workshop and the completion of this report: Telissia Thompson, senior project assistant, skillfully coordinated the workshop logistics and Jamie Casey, project assistant, carefully prepared this report for publication. The subcommittee wants particularly to acknowledge its tremendous gratitude to Michele Ver Ploeg, who was the study director for this workshop. The successful conduct of the workshop and completion of this report are in large part due to Shelly's diligent and skillful efforts. The committee is also grateful to Eugenia Grohman, associate director for reports in the Commission on Behavioral and Social Sciences and Education, for her editing. The Bureau of Labor Statistics, the National Institute of Aging, and TIAA/CREF sponsored the workshop; we are grateful for their support.

This report has been reviewed in draft form by individuals chosen for their diverse perspectives and technical expertise, in accordance with procedures approved by the Report Review Committee of the National Research Council. The purpose of this independent review is to provide candid and critical comments that will assist the institution in making the published report as sound as possible and to ensure that the report meets institutional standards for objectivity, evidence, and responsiveness to the study charge. The review comments and draft manuscript remain confidential to protect the integrity of the deliberative process.

We thank the following individuals for their participation in the review of this report: W. Keith Bryant, Department of Policy Analysis and Management, Cornell University; Paula England, Department of Sociology and Population Studies Center, University of Pennsylvania; Chris Jackson, National Accounts and Environment Division, Statistics Canada, Ottawa; Reed Larson, Department of Human and Community Development, University of Illinois, Champaign/Urbana; Kenneth Shepsle, Department of Government, Harvard University; Frank Stafford, Institute for Social Research, University of Michigan.

Although the individuals listed above provided constructive comments and suggestions, it must be emphasized that responsibility for the final content of this report rests entirely with the authoring committee and the institution.

Julie DaVanzo, *Chair*
Time-Use Workshop Subcommittee
Committee on National Statistics

Contents

1

Introduction

A lthough much is known about how Americans budget their financial resources, very little is known about how Americans budget their time resources. How Americans spend their time is one of the most important and least understood characteristics of the population. For example, remarkably little is known about how retired people spend their time, where young children spend their days, or even whether the amount of time Americans are working is increasing or decreasing.

Data on how Americans spend their time, on the activities in which they participate, on how many hours they participate in each activity and on who they were with at the time are not collected on a regular and on-going basis in the United States. Yet such information on time use could be effectively used to better understand the well-being of the population, social and economic behavior, and the implications of public policies. For example, data on time use can be utilized to improve the coverage of national income and product accounts by measuring the time inputs and outputs in nonmarket production. Such measures are important for achieving more complete production accounts and for understanding the effects of public policies on the labor market. Time-use data are also important for making international comparisons. Improved coverage in national income and product accounts that include measures of nonmarket production will enhance the nation's ability to compare the output and income of the United States with those of other high-income and developing economies. Time-use data can also be used to help understand cultural and social differences across countries.

One measure of a society's well-being is the amount of leisure time people have. Many Americans believe they are experiencing a "time crunch," that they do not have enough time for everything they have to do or want to do. Time-use data could be used to help understand why many Americans feel so short of time by tracking trends in time spent in work and leisure activities.

Data on time allocation can be used to further understanding of individuals' decisions to work or not work for pay and, more generally, decisions on how to allocate time to different activities. These data are also important for understanding the allocation of time and goods among members of households. In addition, better measures of how workers spend their time while working for pay can help improve productivity statistics.

An important social, demographic, and economic trend is that Americans are living longer and spending more time in retirement. Little is known about how retirees spend their time. Such information could be important for understanding the contributions of retirees to economic output, both paid and unpaid or in volunteer activities, in considering the care needs of the elderly and the care the elderly provide for others (spouses or grandchildren), and in understanding the health care and other service needs of the elderly.

One of the most substantial policy changes in the past decade was the elimination of the main social welfare program for poor families, Aid to Families with Dependent Children, ending the entitlement to cash benefits and replacing it with a policy emphasizing work. A question relevant for understanding the consequences of this policy change is how the time allocation among work and family care activities of poor families has changed.

Unlike many other countries, the United States has no regular national surveys of time use, so questions about American "time budgets" are largely based on incomplete data and speculation. Australia and Canada both have regular and comprehensive surveys for collecting time use data on a national basis. A harmonized European time-use survey that will be carried out in almost 20 countries is also moving forward through Eurostat.

President Clinton's proposed budget for fiscal 2001 includes funds for the Bureau of Labor Statistics (BLS) to develop a survey to measure how Americans spend their time (U.S. Department of Labor, 2000). BLS has already explored the feasibility of such a survey. In 1997, a pilot study that collected time-use data for a sample of Americans was conducted, and the results of that study were presented at a 1997 conference sponsored by BLS and the MacArthur Network on the Family and the Economy. Using knowledge gained from the pilot study and the conference, BLS published a report on the feasibility of a national time-use survey and developed a proposal to conduct the survey (Horrigan et al., 1999).

With the release of the BLS feasibility report and proposal and with renewed interest in time-use data and research, the Committee on National Statistics of the National Research Council held a workshop to consider data and methodological issues in measuring time use. The workshop brought together experts in the fields of survey methodology, demography, economics, psychology, sociology, and statistics. Representatives from BLS presented their report on the feasibility of a national time-use survey. Other papers presented at the workshop covered four broad topics: (1) theories of time allocation and public policy considerations, (2) applications of time-use data, (3) accounting for nonmarket household production in national accounts, and (4) approaches to measuring time use. The workshop also included two roundtable discussions—one on conceptual issues in measuring time use and one on future research priorities. See Appendix A for the workshop agenda; summaries of the papers presented at the workshop are in Appendix B.

This document summarizes the workshop, drawing on the presented papers and the formal discussions of them and on general discussions at the workshop. The next chapter discusses why time-use data are needed, highlighting many of the policy and behavioral applications of time-use data introduced above. Next, the report summarizes conceptual issues covered during the workshop. This chapter includes discussion of a framework for how individuals and households allocate their time and a commentary on some conceptual issues in measuring time use—specifically, in defining work and leisure activities, measuring time spent simultaneously in multiple activities, and valuing time. Chapter 4 summarizes time-use studies that have been carried out in the United States, as well as the time-use studies that other countries have conducted. Chapter 5 summarizes the discussion of methods for collecting time-use data, sampling issues in using diaries to collect time-use data, and the importance of ensuring that the data collected match the uses for which the data are intended. Chapter 6 covers features of the proposed BLS time-use survey and a summary of discussants' comments on the proposal. Chapter 7 summarizes the common themes that emerged at the workshop.

This workshop summary is not intended to provide a complete account of all the behavioral and policy issues that can be better informed with data on time allocation. There are important topical areas for which time-use data could be used that were not covered in the papers and discussion of the workshop, and so are not covered in this summary. For example, there are many potential uses for time-use data in the private sector. Marketers often want to know when and how often Americans use different forms of media so that marketing campaigns can be more effectively directed. Retailers may want to know how the Internet is shaping patterns in time spent shopping. Employers certainly have an interest in better understanding how employees use their time at work and how employees spend time working for pay when they are at home or off-site.

Time-use data can also be used for public policy issues that were not discussed at the workshop. For example, time-use data can improve understanding of the use of and needs for, publicly provided goods, such as parks, recreational facilities, roads, and mass transit systems. Patterns of use of such public goods can help governments and regional planners design future transportation systems, zoning, and recreational facilities.

Within the topics of methodological and statistical issues for measuring time use and the proposed BLS time-use survey, the workshop was not intended to provide a definitive review of all the methodological and statistical issues in measuring time use, nor to give the BLS specific guidance in planning its time-use survey. Moreover, workshop participants did not agree on all methodological considerations. For example, there was substantial disagreement between participants about recall error and how long survey respondents can accurately remember what they did on a previous day. Yet there were broad areas of agreement with regard to the importance for time-use data collection and with regard to the need to consider certain methodological approaches in future time-use surveys; the final chapter summarizes these common themes.

2

The Importance of Time-Use Data

There is a wide range of potential uses of data on how Americans spend their time, including understanding the effects of public policies on individual behavior. For example, low-income workers are sometimes eligible to receive subsidized child care. Time-use data can help in understanding how these policies affect the amount of time that parents spend working at home or outside the home and how much time they spend with their children. Aside from public policy uses, time-use data can improve our understanding of individual and household behavior, especially with respect to time allocation decisions and in improving our knowledge of the well-being of the nation. In this chapter, important functions of time-use data for informing public policy and for better understanding of behavior and well-being are discussed.

TIME-USE DATA FOR PUBLIC POLICY

This chapter focuses on five potential ways in which time-use data can be used for public policy: (1) to expand the national economic accounts; (2) to understand the transition from work to unemployment (and vice versa) and from work to retirement and the time spent working for pay during "retirement"; (3) to document time spent in market, nonmarket, and leisure activities; (4) to document and understand decisions that individuals make about how much time they spend caring for children and for other family members; and (5) to understand the effects of recent major changes in social welfare programs. Linda Waite, Thomas Juster, Sandra Hofferth, and Steven

Landefeld presented papers that covered these issues. This section looks first at the national income accounts, issues of work and retirement, child care, and welfare reform and then considers issues of well-being more broadly.

Augmented National Economic Accounts

A primary public policy use of time-use data is to enhance the coverage of National Income and Product Accounts (NIPA). The NIPA accounts provide measures of economic activity for the nation and are the principal means of measuring growth in the nation's economy over time and in comparing income and production across countries. The NIPA accounts almost exclusively measure only market production and, hence, do not take into account goods and services—such as the production and consumption of meals at home—that a household produces for its own private consumption or for any household production that is not traded in the formal market but is consumed by others, such as giving a neighbor fresh tomatoes from your garden.

A goal of the accounts is to comprehensively tabulate all economic activity in the nation (Landefeld and McCulla, 1999). The exclusion of nonmarket production has been noted for many years.[1] Nonmarket production has not been included in part because there are conceptual and practical issues in measuring these activities. Conceptual issues include classifying a nonmarket activity as a productive activity, valuing the output produced, and valuing the time inputs needed to produce it. (These issues are discussed further in the Chapter 3 of the report.) A practical issue that is a barrier to measuring nonmarket output in national accounts is the lack of consistently and regularly produced data on how much time is spent in nonmarket activities. Landefeld and McCulla (1999:27) argue that the "greatest barrier to constructing a consistent set of time series on the value of household production is the lack of consistent data on time-use, both for current and earlier periods."

What policy questions could be better informed if time-use data were available to use in the NIPA accounts? Participants at the workshop emphasized the following areas:

• What have been the trends in the number of hours worked? Are data on hours for which pay is received a good reflection of true hours worked? Are measures of labor productivity reliable?
• How much of the historic increase in the U.S. gross domestic product

---

[1]Landefeld and McCulla (1999) briefly chronicle the interest in including nonmarket production in national income accounts.

(GDP) is due to the increased labor force participation of women and how much was in fact offset by a reduction in nonmarket activity?

• How much household time use should be classified and measured as "investment," such as time spent helping a child with homework as an investment in the child's future well-being, and how does that factor into national accounting?

• How do the national income levels of less developed countries compare with those of more developed countries when nonmarket time is accounted for?

• How do tax policies and other government policies, such as subsidized child care and education loan and tax breaks, affect labor market and nonmarket time use?

Significant efforts to include nonremunerated work into national income accounts are under way in other countries. Estimates of household production output and the inputs used for the outputs have been made in Australia, Canada, and three Scandinavian countries—Finland, Sweden and Norway (Ironmonger, 1997). The Bureau of Economic Analysis in the U.S. has also produced household output and input tables (Landefeld and McCulla, 1999), but these estimates are not currently used in "core" GDP figures. Rather, the estimates are used in satellite accounts to the national income accounts, which measure production typically not included in the standard set of national accounts.

Results from the Landefeld and McCulla study provide a valuable example of how time-use data can be used. Using data from the 1980s, the study adjusts GDP from 1946 to 1997 by including measures of nonmarket household production and by counting household expenditures on consumer durables as investment. One particularly interesting result is that the growth in total nominal output for 1946-1997 would be estimated at a 7.1 percent annual rate instead of the official 7.3 percent annual rate when nonmarket production is included and household durables are treated as investment in GDP. The authors argue that the lower growth figures reflect a decrease in nonmarket production over the five decades largely due to an increase in female labor force participation. The GDP in 1946 increases by 43 percent when household production is included, but only by 24 percent in 1997. When expenditures on household durables are treated as investment, GDP increases by 5 percent in 1946 and by 8 percent in 1997.

In the future, more countries will be producing such satellite accounts. Perhaps the biggest boost to these efforts will come from the Eurostat harmonized time-use survey involving 18 countries, which will be used to produce such tables. As more and more countries develop the data for measuring nonmarket production, methods for dealing with some of the conceptual issues in measuring nonmarket production will evolve. In addition, the value of the data for making cross-country comparisons will increase.

Work and Retirement

Time Use at Work

Time-use data can be used to improve measures of how time is spent at work or while working for pay and to understand the effects of public policy on labor market and job outcomes. Technological gains are allowing more work to be done away from the office and have contributed to the blurring of the lines between work in the market, nonmarket work, and leisure. Time spent at the "workplace" may not entirely consist of time spent in market work; it may also include time spent in nonmarket work or leisure. Likewise, time spent away from the "workplace" or at home may include market work time. Conventional measures of time spent at work—which are usually collected through recorded hours of work from company or organizational payroll records or through stylized questions asking the amount of time respondents typically spend at work—are unlikely to fully capture the blurring of these lines and do not provide detail of what "work" is being done. Such information is important because better data on time use while on the job can help improve productivity measures and can contribute to understanding how technological innovations have affected productivity.

The Transition from Work to Unemployment and Retirement

Another area of public policy for which time-use data can be used to better inform policy making is in understanding transitions between paid work and nonmarket work, volunteerism, unemployment, and retirement. This includes an individual's choice of how many hours to spend in paid work and other activities and how public policy affects individuals' use of time, in contrast to measures of the aggregate levels discussed in the previous section. Some of the policy questions raised in the previous section apply here as well. For example, one question is how tax and employment policies, such as the Earned Income Tax Credit, family leave policies, and subsidized child care, affect household decisions regarding how much to work in the home or in the market for pay.

The tradeoff between household work and market work has been studied by economists, sociologists and policy analysts for a long time and there is an extensive literature on the topic. There are, however, other alternatives to household work (besides leisure) for those who do not work full time for pay, as workshop participants Thomas Juster and Linda Waite discussed. One of these is volunteerism, which is of particular interest for understanding how older and retired adults spend their time (Hill et al., 1999). Of policy interest here are how wage, tax, Social Security, and other policies affect volunteer time, how volunteer time translates into the production of goods and services, the social or community capital that is built from volunteerism (see Juster, 1999; Smeeding, 1997; and Hill et al. 1999), the personal satisfaction and health benefits that accrue to the volunteers, and how policies might affect the amount of volunteering.

Nonmarket activity also includes educational or training activities, either fulltime or while working. Public education from kindergarten through high school (K-12), subsidized public colleges, and federal and state grant and loan programs for college students and educational tax credits are all publicly funded investments to develop skills and to train current and future employees. How policies affect time spent in these activities is an important question on an individual level. Discussant Suzanne Bianchi also noted that examining how elementary and secondary school children spend their time in educational activities is a key to understanding educational outcomes, both on an individual level and at the school level. For example, a study of children's time use at school could provide information on how different classroom settings and schedules affect the cognitive development of children. Measures of time spent in learning and training activities outside the formal educational system could also prove useful. The productivity outcomes of time spent in on-the-job training might be used to better inform learning and training policies for workers. Each of these kinds of studies would require longitudinal data on time use and extensive data on the characteristics of respondents. Throughout the entire formal educational system, it is also important to understand how time investments pay off in terms of future earnings and productivity gains on an aggregate level, as Dale Jorgenson pointed out in his discussion. Time-series data on time use in educational activities are required for this type of research.

People who are not in the paid work force may be unemployed and looking for work. Time-use data can help researchers and policy makers understand how much time unemployed persons spend looking for jobs, how much they work in the informal sector, and in general, how they spend their time while unemployed. Of policy interest is how unemployment benefits and the timing of benefit coverage affect these decisions.

The time use of those who are disabled is also of policy interest, as Joseph Altonji pointed out in his discussion. The types of policy questions discussed include:

- Has the Americans with Disabilities Act increased work time for the disabled?
- Have public accommodations for the disabled increased their work participation?

• How do those who receive disability payments or Supplemental Security Income (SSI) payments spend their time?

Each of these policy questions could be informed with data on the time use of disabled people.

Time-use data are also of policy interest for understanding transitions to retirement and how retirees spend their time. As Americans live longer and as some Americans retire earlier, it becomes important to know what retirees do with their time (Waite and Nielsen, 1999). When an individual retires, he or she may still work for pay or engage in unpaid work activities. Retirement for many may actually mean a change in a career, a move to part-time work for pay, or work as a volunteer. How social security, Medicare, and other policies for older adults affect these decisions is of particular interest for policy development.

Child and Family Care

For many people, a primary component of nonmarket work is time spent caring for others. This is especially true for parents with young children. For many elderly couples, one spouse often needs assistance or care that is often provided by the other spouse. Likewise, the children of elderly parents often provide care for their parents. Workshop participants discussed several policy considerations that could be informed by data on time spent in care-taking or care-receiving activities. One example is how subsidized child care for low-income families affects parents' time spent working for pay. Another example is how child outcomes (educational achievement or test scores, for example) are affected by the time parents spend with children (Hofferth, 1999).

Also important to policy is the degree to which individuals substitute their own time caring for relatives with the time of market-provided care-givers and what factors determine how much time is spent caring for a relative or spouse. A related issue is whether the health and general well-being outcomes of those who are receiving the care are better when the care is provided by a relative as opposed to when care is given by a market provider. In her discussion, Rebecca Blank identified several other issues. For example, the question of how the care that older adults receive from their spouse or another relative interact with policies of the health care system is relevant for policy discussions about giving tax breaks for those who care for relatives. Similarly, as different types of health care systems are debated, it would be useful to know how different health institutional structures support family care.

Welfare Reform

The wide-sweeping changes to the main federal cash assistance program to low income families with children in 1996 have many implications for how recipients of cash assistance spend their time. In contrast to the old system, the new system requires most of those receiving assistance to engage in work or work-related activities in order to receive assistance. How current recipients, former recipients, and potential recipients spend their time and how this relates to their outcomes (earnings, program participation, and well-being) and their children's outcomes are major policy questions. Of particular interest is what these families are doing to support themselves in terms of market and nonmarket activities.

An ethnographic study by Edin and Lein (1997) indicates that under the old program rules, many welfare recipients worked both in the formal market (although earnings from such work would reduce benefits) and informally (where work income was supposed to be, but was not always, reported). The incentives for devoting time in the formal labor market have changed under the new program rules. The entitlement for cash assistance was eliminated and most recipients must now participate in work or work-related activities to receive assistance. Time-use data can help policy analysts understand behavioral responses to the new incentives. As Rebecca Blank stated at the workshop, an important part of evaluating welfare reform is understanding how the new work requirements affect a segment of the population that previously received public assistance and worked less than they now do.

TIME-USE DATA FOR UNDERSTANDING WELL-BEING

Collecting time-use data on how retirees spend their time and on how much time Americans spend in educational activities or in volunteer activities need not be justified only for policy purposes. It is also important to know how Americans use time in order to have a better understanding of the well-being of the nation, including the degree to which people feel time-crunched or experience stress due to having too little time to do the things they want to do. This section discusses how time-use data can improve understanding of well-being in the United States.

Recently there has been some debate on whether Americans are working more hours than they have previously and whether Americans are spending fewer years in the work force than they did in the past. Part of the reason this debate has not been settled is that there are inadequate data on the number of hours that people work for pay (Smeeding, 1997). Data on how Americans use their time are not produced regularly and have not been produced since

1985.   Interesting questions could be addressed with such data. For example, as the American population ages, it would be interesting to track changes in time use. If Americans are spending fewer years in the labor force, is it because people retire earlier, as some workshop participants suggested, or is it because more and more young adults are going to college, delaying full-time entry into the paid labor force for several years, and because many middle-aged Americans are going back to college or receiving additional training, which takes them out of the full-time labor force, as other participants suggested?

Collecting time-use data will augment knowledge on these types of trends. Time-use data will also help researchers and policy makers understand what retirees do when they leave the labor force and can provide data on the educational and training activities in which individuals participate. It will also be useful to know how time use varies over business cycles as the unemployment rate rises and falls. Measures of time use on the job would be extremely useful for research on labor productivity. Most broadly, time-use data will be valuable for describing what people do when they are not at work.

Time-use data can provide interesting assessments of noneconomic measures of well-being. In past time-use studies, respondents have been asked to describe their satisfaction levels from different activities and their emotional states during those activities. These subjective measures of intrinsic satisfaction associated with time spent in different activities can be used to better understand well-being. Time diary studies and experiential sampling method (ESM) studies (both are described below) have both been used to better understand subjective satisfaction from work, leisure, and other activities.

The hours during which work activities take place may also affect well-being and have implications for quality of life. Daniel Hamermesh, in his discussion, showed results from his recent study examining the hours of the day during which people work and how that has changed over the past 25 years (Hamermesh, 1999). In comparison with 25 years ago, he found that workers are working more during the middle of the day (between 6 a.m. and 6 p.m.), than during evening or nighttime hours. Many would argue that a movement away from working during the middle of the night towards working standard hours is an improvement in the quality of life. This finding is one example of how time-use data can improve the richness of measures of well-being.

The growing disparity in income and earnings across the population has received a great deal of attention in policy and research communities. One aspect of well-being that is not usually a part of these discussions is whether there is a large disparity in the amount and timing of leisure. For example, one person may be "money rich, but time poor," a phrase used to describe those who are monetarily wealthy but have little time away from work to devote to leisure. Another person may be "time rich, but money poor," a term used for those who have more leisure time and relatively less money.[2] While standard economic measures of well-being would classify the first individual as better off, if differences in leisure time are counted, the first individual may not look as well off. Time-use data can at least help describe who has leisure time and what hours they have it.

Related to the issue of well-being is the issue of the "time crunch." The time crunch is generally used to describe the condition of those who feel as if they do not have enough time to do the things they need and want to do. For many individuals, the time crunch raises the level of stress in their lives, which may in turn have negative effects on their physical and mental health, work performance, or family relations. Others may not experience such tangible negative effects of the time crunch, but may instead feel that their quality of life is not as good as it was or could be. Workshop participants argued that understanding these trends in how people feel about their use of time or lack of time for leisure activities can give a more complete picture of the quality of life and changes in the quality of life in the United States. Time-use data with information on perceptions of time use (for example, how quickly time passes or how stressful an activity was) and on time spent in activities can help analysts decipher what activities or schedules make people feel time crunched or what activities are taking up time.

These are some of the major uses of time-use data for informing public policy and for furthering knowledge of the well-being of the nation. There are, of course, many other public policy questions that could benefit from time-use data, as well as many private uses of time-use data. For example, marketers would like to know when certain demographic groups are watching television or listening to the radio. Businesses may want to keep on top of consumer shopping trends (e.g., the time of day or the day of the week consumers typically shop, by demographic category). Also, as Rebecca Blank pointed out, employers could use detailed time-use data on how their employees use their time when setting personnel policies.

Workshop participants emphasized the potential applications of time-use data for understanding behavior and well-being and for informing public policy. There are, however, limitations of time-use data for these purposes. For example, time has shortcomings as a metric as it is not easy to put a value on time.[3] Individual skills, ambition, and intelligence determine how productive a person is in different activities. Measuring time spent in activities is subject to these differences in productivity (i.e., some people are more pro-

---

[2]See Michael (1996) for an introduction to the topic and National Research Council (1995) for a summary of implications of the topic for conceptualizing and measuring poverty.

[3]See Michael (1996) for a discussion of the issues in using time as a metric.

ductive than others in a given period for a given activity). Furthermore, classifying activities in which people spend their time can be difficult, and it is often difficult to classify, measure, and value the outputs of these activities. These limitations present conceptual and measurement challenges for time-use researchers. These challenges arose during the workshop discourse and are discussed in the next chapter of the report.

3

Conceptual Issues

Measuring the well-being of the population is essential to understanding the effects of public policies. One common measure of well-being is the value of the consumption of marketed goods and services, such as food, shelter, and recreation. A common theme at the workshop was that a broader concept of well-being should include the consumption of nonmarket goods and services. To do so requires data on how much time is spent producing goods and services not sold in the market. This chapter discusses some of the conceptual issues surrounding how people allocate their time towards different activities (both market and nonmarket), how activities are measured, and how time spent in nonmarket activities is valued.

GENERAL CONCEPTUAL APPROACH

The framework usually used to describe time allocation decisions assumes that people allocate time among alternative uses to satisfy their needs and desires. In economic language, individuals allocate time between leisure and work (both market and nonmarket work) subject to income and time constraints and according to their preferences for goods and the satisfactions provided by different uses of time.

On careful examination, classifying time into market work, nonmarket work, and leisure is a difficult conceptual and operational issue. Market work usually is meant to refer to work done for pay. Yet, as workshop participants discussed, not all time spent at "work" is devoted to job-related activities. Some time is devoted to personal maintenance, such as eating and grooming.

Some time is devoted to nonmarket production, such as searching for a plumber to fix a household problem. Some time is devoted to purely leisure activities, such as talking about yesterday's football game with a colleague or checking the Internet for movie schedules. Furthermore, as work schedules become more flexible and more market work is conducted at home, the lines between market work, nonmarket work, and leisure may become even more blurred. Although it may be possible to measure time use distinctively enough to separate nonmarket work from market work while at work, many activities can be classified as both work and leisure. And, people sometimes receive enjoyment or satisfaction from doing their jobs, which complicates how work is conceptualized.

Nonmarket work is typically thought of as unpaid time devoted to activities that produce a "commodity," such as cooking, house cleaning, or mowing the lawn. Nonmarket work and leisure can also be intertwined. For example, gardening is a nonmarket activity that produces a tangible output, such as tomatoes, that can be sold in the market or consumed by the gardener. Gardening may also be a leisure activity, as the gardener may enjoy the process of growing the tomatoes, working with the soil, or enjoying the outdoors. Nonmarket outputs are often difficult to measure, both conceptually and operationally. Although the outputs to cooking and cleaning are easily measured conceptually, such as the number of clean shirts and the number of cooked hamburgers, some household activities do not have easily measured outputs, for example, caring for a relative or reading to one's child (a point we discuss further below in the section on valuing time).

Most standard approaches to economic valuation assume that leisure time provides satisfaction to an individual that work and other productive activities do not, but several studies challenge this assumption. University of Michigan studies in 1975-1976 and 1982-1982 asked respondents to rate the level of intrinsic enjoyment they received from many activities throughout the day, on a scale from zero to ten (Juster, 1985). Respondents gave high enjoyment rankings not only to activities for which there were interactions with children, but also for paid work activities. They gave low rankings for activities involving household work. In surveys by Robinson and Godbey (1997), time spent at work gave respondents more satisfaction than time spent at many nonmarket and leisure activities, suggesting that time spent at work may not be all disutility—indeed, it may not be "work."[1]

Similarly, individuals may receive direct benefits from nonmarket work activities. As noted above, gardening (or fishing) may be a means of produc-

---

[1] As Pollak (1999) notes, these measures of satisfaction are measures of total or overall satisfaction; not marginal satisfaction, or the change in satisfaction due to a change in the amount of time spent working.

ing food. However, they may also be activities that yield direct satisfaction. In many cases, the value of the fishing is likely to far exceed the value of the fish.

Tom Juster proposed a conceptual definition of activities to distinguish those that are work (both market and nonmarket) from those that are leisure. The proposed distinction is determined by whether the activities provide or produce extrinsic rewards or intrinsic rewards. Extrinsic rewards are the results or products of activities that produce *future* utility or satisfaction. For example, market work has extrinsic rewards because a worker receives income that is used for future consumption; similarly, doing laundry has extrinsic rewards of producing clean sheets. Intrinsic rewards (also called "process benefits") result from activities that provide direct utility or satisfaction (Juster, 1999). For example, a drive to look at the autumn leaves is intrinsically rewarding; it is not taken to actually go anywhere (indeed, such an activity almost always goes in a circle).

As workshop participants noted, these distinctions are not always clear. Hiking may be immediately rewarding in body and spirit, but the physical activity may also provide future health benefits. Although people may work primarily for the extrinsic reward of wages and benefits, work may provide intrinsic rewards if, for example, workers enjoy interacting with their coworkers. Reading to a child may have intrinsic rewards in that it provides direct satisfaction. It may also have extrinsic rewards in that it improves a child's verbal ability and is an "investment" in his or her future.

The degree to which an activity has intrinsic or extrinsic rewards or costs may also depend on the time of the day of the activity and its sequence in relation to other activities. For example, if someone dreads going to work, a 20-minute walk *to* work might have lower intrinsic rewards than a 20-minute walk home *from* work at the end of the day. Likewise, a call from a good friend very early in the morning may have fewer intrinsic rewards than a call from the same friend in the evening. The intrinsic and extrinsic rewards of an activity may also depend upon who else is present for the activity. Having dinner alone versus having dinner with one's spouse will likely have different intrinsic rewards. Each of these examples underscore the conceptual factors that complicate classification of activities as either intrinsically or extrinsically rewarding.

The discussion on how to define activities has implications for data collection, a point we briefly mention here, but discuss further in Chapter 5. For example, if shared time with family members and loved ones is an important part of the intrinsic rewards of an activity, as some evidence indicates (Bryant and Zick, 1996a; Bryant and Wang, 1990), then it is important to also gather information on who else was present during an activity or to collect data on multiple household members. It might also be useful to understand respondents' satisfaction level while they participate in the activities to get a better sense of why they engage in the activity, in the hope that intrinsically rewarding activities can be better distinguished from extrinsically rewarding activities. Similarly, it is important to collect contextual data about an activity, such as where the activity took place, at what time of day, and who else was there, to understand satisfaction and the intrinsic rewards of activities. Because these issues cut across the fields of psychology, sociology, and economics, understanding them requires an interdisciplinary approach involving all the behavioral disciplines, as discussant Nancy Folbre noted.

HOUSEHOLD TIME USE

The theories that have been developed to understand how individuals and households allocate their time among activities to produce and consume commodities and what affects this allocation depend on clear definitions, conceptually and operationally, of the inputs and outputs of the process. Household production theory assumes that households engage in productive activities that use as inputs market goods and services, the time of household members, and household capital stock. These inputs are used either to produce satisfaction or utility directly or to produce other goods and services that in turn produce future utility or satisfaction.[2] The theory covers a wide range of goods and services produced by the household—cleaning, cooking, caring for children and other relatives, recreation, procreation, and education, to name a few.

In a formal model, preferences of the household (or for multiple person households, preferences of the individual members in the household in combination with intrahousehold bargaining) determine *what* is produced. For example, a household that likes to barbeque and have a place to sit outdoors may decide to build a deck. The household must also decide *how* to build the deck, by family labor, through a market contractor, or by barter for household services. One important determinant is the cost of outside labor in comparison with the subjective value, or "shadow price," of household labor. Other determinants are the skills of the householder and capital requirements. Households generally produce their own dishwashing services but seldom produce their own cardiovascular surgery services. Likewise, a household may have the capital and technology available to produce a meal for several people, but probably not for a hundred people. This "make or buy" decision is a complicated function of prices and skills, of which the price of the time and the quality of the output are two of the central determinants.

However, as Robert A. Pollak pointed out in his paper, there are several complications to the theory of household production, related to defining the

---

[2]The centerpiece of household production theory is Becker's 1965 article.

commodities and dealing with simultaneous activities. To continue the example of building a deck, household members may get satisfaction out of working with their hands and generally enjoy building the deck themselves. In other words, in addition to receiving extrinsic benefits from the completed project, the builder may also receive intrinsic rewards, or process benefits, from engaging in the activity. Two goods are produced, the deck and the satisfaction from the process of building it. Ignoring the process benefits ignores some of the utility derived by the household. This example shows that while the outputs produced by a firm are usually fairly easy to measure, the outputs produced by a household are often hard to measure, and the intrinsic benefits of household time use (including time for work done for pay) are almost always extremely difficult to assess.

One way time-use data and household production theory have been used together is to try to understand how parental time spent with children affects a child's outcomes. Understanding how the inputs of this activity (time, capital stock, and market goods) affect the output is a very interesting question. It requires data on the inputs to the process, meaning that time-use data should be collected in addition to data on other inputs used in the process. In her remarks, discussant Jeanne Brooks-Gunn stated that in doing so, it is important to clearly differentiate activities in categories as much as possible. For example, learning activities should be differentiated from playing activities. Understanding how parental time affects child outcomes also requires clearly measured outputs. Yet even with clearly measured outputs and inputs, it may be difficult to separate any effects of parents' time with their children from unmeasured characteristics of the parents that also contribute to children's outcomes (Pollak, 1999).

Other workshop participants stressed that it is important to collect comprehensive information on the inputs used for household production. Discussant Jack Triplett noted that information on the time and other inputs used in producing outputs in the household can also help improve measures of prices and output in the service economy. Triplett used the example of banks that provide ATM services to customers, which save time for the customers. In valuing the output of ATMs, Triplett argues that it is important to have some information on how much time is saved, by whom, and when it is saved, and the valuation of that time. Nancy Folbre emphasized the need for data on inputs and human capital of household members in order to better understand household production processes.

Time-use data are also valuable for furthering understanding of how household members allocate their time and goods. The theory of intrahousehold allocation postulates that who does what in the household is a function of the value of time of individual household members, as well as the household's wealth and capital stock and the skills, preferences, and bargaining power of household members. For some household time-use activities, one household member's time could be substituted for another household members time. For example, one spouse can do the laundry while the other spouse goes to the store for groceries. The combined productivity from both activities is likely to be higher if one spouse does one activity while the other spouse does another. Yet, for some activities, spousal time use may be complementary, that is, there are gains to having both spouses present for the activity, such as the example given above of a husband and wife dining together.

Another interesting application of time-use data is to examine intra-household allocation of time and goods. One example involves the allocation of housework among male and female adults in a household. One reason that women do more housework might be because they have a stronger preference for a cleaner house than men; another might be that men have more "power" than women and allocate the unpleasant tasks to women. It may be possible to test these hypotheses with time-use data by looking at the time that *one-person* male and female households spend cleaning (controlling for other variables and differences in values of time). However, differences in housework by males and females in single-person households might not reflect preference structures; they might instead reflect the attempt by women to build "gender human capital" that can be used in the marriage market: that is, a single woman may cook to make herself more attractive to potential spouses. Or, people in single-person households might be inherently different from those in multiperson households in ways that are correlated with their time use so that the results from single-person households cannot be directly applied to multiperson households. At the very least, the availability of time-use data can provide descriptive measures of how people and households allocate their time and how variations in technology, wage rates, and prices affect those activities.

VALUATION OF HOUSEHOLD PRODUCTION AND TIME USE

A primary conceptual issue in measuring nonmarket output of households is in identifying the nonmarket outputs, that is, identifying the output of a nonmarket activity as a production activity rather than a consumption activity. Some commodities are easily identified, such as a home-cooked meal, which has a clear input and a measurable output. Other commodities and activities are less clearly defined. For example, reading a story to one's child could be classified as a leisure activity for both the parent and the child. It could also be classified as a production activity, either as a child care activity or an activity to further the child's development (or both). Viewed as a productive activity, the parent is providing a service that, while not purchased, is nonetheless consumed by the child. The service the parent provides could be sold in the market. But the reading is only one component of the service provided by the parent for her own child; the joint activity also includes the parent and the child spending time together. It is this additional benefit (output) of the activity that is not easily classified, measured, or valued.

Assuming output can be defined, another conceptual dilemma in measuring the nonmarket output of households is how to value the output produced. One approach is to use a price measure of the output produced. In other words, assign a dollar amount to the output produced by a household that is equal to the amount for which the output could be sold in the market (which would have to be estimated by the price of a proxy good or service that is actually sold in the market). However, as Landefeld and McCulla (1999) note, the producer of the household good is often also the consumer, so there is no transaction. Furthermore, some household outputs could not be sold in the market and therefore have no good proxy measure, as in the parent-child example in the previous paragraph.

The other approach is to value household outputs by adding the costs of inputs used to produce the output. Nonmarket production, like market production, is a process of taking existing goods and services, existing capital stock, and the time and ability of a producer to create an output (product). Valuing the intermediate goods and services and capital stock used to produce a nonmarket commodity is not a difficult task conceptually (although the actual measuring might be). The goods for inputs purchased by households are already included in the national income and product accounts. However, valuing the labor time used to produce a commodity is a difficult task that requires making assumptions about an individual's value of time spent in nonmarket activities.

There are two general methods for valuing time spent in nonmarket and leisure activities: the opportunity cost approach and the market cost approach. The opportunity cost approach is based on the view that individuals allocate their time so that the value of an additional hour spent in market work activity is equal to the value of an additional hour spent in nonmarket or leisure activities. To "buy" one more hour of time in nonmarket activities, one must give up the pay from one additional hour of work for pay. This approach uses an individual's post-tax hourly wage rate as a measure of the value of an hour of market and nonmarket time. The opportunity cost approach is conceptually and operationally appealing, and it is consistent with economic theory. Moreover, wage rates of employed individuals are fairly easy to obtain from survey data.

Workshop participants noted some complications to this approach, however. First, people who do not work for pay have no wages to measure. For them, the "reservation wage" or wage rate at which the person is indifferent to working or not working may be the relevant wage rate to use. However, the reservation wage rate is not observed and therefore, not easily measured. It is also not at all clear how to measure the opportunity cost of time for children, who obviously do not work for pay. Another complication of the opportunity cost approach is that it ignores any intrinsic reward or process benefits gained from activities. Nonmarket time spent taking out the garbage may have process costs while market work may have process benefits. If the wage rate is used to value the time spent in both types of activities, it implicitly assumes the process benefits for both activities (and across all other activities) are the same. A more practical concern with the opportunity cost approach is that it also assumes that people can allocate exactly the number of hours they wish to work. In reality, hours of work are often fixed by custom or law, and in many salaried jobs the marginal pay for an additional hour of work (above 40 hours of work) is generally zero, at least in the short run. Finally, wage rates do not account for any fringe benefits a worker may receive, which may distort the wage rate as a measure of one's opportunity cost of time.

The market cost approach to valuing time uses the wage rate of a substitute provider of the activity. For example, to value an hour spent building a deck, the market wage rate of a carpenter would be used. In its simplest form, this method has the shortcoming of assuming that there are no quality differences in a deck built by a carpenter and a deck built by the householder. To get around this issue, the wage rate of a generalist is used rather than the wage rate of a specialist: in other words, the wage rate of a handyman is used instead of the wage rate of a specialist carpenter. For the market cost approach, as in the opportunity cost approach, any process benefits are ignored. The net effect may be to understate the value of a home-produced good because it does not account for any process benefits the household obtains from the activity (Landefeld and McCulla, 1999).

These conceptual issues have been understood for many years, and no easy resolutions have been proposed. It is clear that further efforts to define and measure activities, to value activities, and to develop better models of how individuals and households allocate their time are needed. Time-use data, with clear definitions of activities, identification of simultaneous activities (see below), contextual data on who else is present during the activity, measures of inputs used in household production processes, and information on wage rates of the respondents, will aid in the resolution or refinement of these conceptual issues.

SIMULTANEOUS ACTIVITIES

At any time, an individual may be engaged in more than one activity. It is possible to cook dinner and watch a child at the same time (or at least be "on call" if the child needs help). Similarly, one can watch television and fold laundry at the same time, or read a newspaper while riding on the train. Even if a perfect classification system for activities that could separate work from leisure was developed, it would still be difficult to separate activities conducted simultaneously, or jointly. Ignoring these simultaneous activities will miss many daily activities. Therefore, it is important to consider the different approaches to measuring time spent in simultaneous activities. Some of the alternatives are reviewed in Nordhaus (1999).

One method for measuring time spent in joint activities is to count an hour spent jointly doing two activities as two hours. That is, jointly folding laundry and watching television for an hour would be measured as an hour of folding laundry and an hour of watching television. This approach is unsatisfactory, however, because it does not satisfy the constraint that a day has 24 hours. Moreover, it is likely that the number of hours of activities would increase as surveys became more detailed. The method also presumes the amount of laundry folded per minute while watching television is the same as the amount of laundry folded per minute of time spent solely folding laundry.

Another approach is to count only one of the simultaneous activities, which involves a determination (by the respondent or by the analyst) of which activity is the primary activity or the one that is more important. Most surveys of time use have asked respondents to designate a primary activity and a secondary activity. Usually, respondents are asked to report what they are doing at a certain time and whether they were doing anything else at the same time. The primary activity is then classified as what the respondent first reported, and the secondary activity is what the respondent reported doing in addition to the primary one. In accounting for hours spent in a day, only the time spent in the primary activity is counted; the sum of secondary activities may be counted and tabulated separately. Counting only primary activities in producing statistics on daily totals of time use in different activities would not count many meaningful activities that are likely to be reported as secondary activities. For example, a family may eat a meal together and spend the meal discussing the day's activities. Most likely, the primary activity the respondent lists would be eating, and the secondary activity would be visiting with family members. However, as Julie DaVanzo noted, the actual eating part may take only a few minutes, while the visiting takes more time and may be the more interesting activity to total and report. Essentially, the problem is that the respondent or the analyst must designate one activity as the primary activity and the other activity as the secondary activity. Inevitably, analysis will correctly or incorrectly focus on those activities designated as primary activities when the secondary activity may also be of interest.

A third approach is to create compound activities—that is, to define a joint activity as a distinct activity. For example, an hour spent visiting with the family while eating dinner would be a separate activity from visiting and from eating. While this approach is conceptually appealing, it may lead to an enormous number of activities (although, the number of compound activities used in the classification scheme could be limited to a few of particular relevance for a survey). It would also complicate tabulations to the extent that the compound activity combined two types of higher level classifications (such as work and leisure).

A fourth approach may apply to certain activities that are recorded by a respondent as simultaneous, but are in fact distinct and sequential. These distinct activities may be aggregated over in the survey and can be called "multiplexed" activities. (This term refers to a process of transmitting several messages or signals simultaneously on the same channel.) That is, one is either talking or listening but not doing both at once. Or to continue a previous example, one is either folding laundry or watching television, but not actually doing both at the same time. If one could just slice up time finely enough (which is not an easy task), the multiple activities would become short bursts of solo activities. A survey could ask respondents to report what they were doing in 5-minute or even 1-minute intervals to distinguish two separate activities that may be reported as simultaneous activities if 15 minute intervals were used instead. So, for example, 15 minutes of folding laundry and watching television might be divided into 10 minutes of folding laundry and 5 minutes of watching television. This approach may work for some studies that require such detail. However, this method puts a huge burden on respondents to recall very fine intervals of time use. Most time diaries allow respondents to designate their own intervals for this reason. Furthermore, there are some activities for which this approach would not work because they are intrinsically simultaneous (such as reading while traveling on a train) and cannot be separated at however fine a slice of time. Riding the train does not exclude one from also reading, conversing, or sleeping. Both activities can truly be conducted simultaneously.

Another approach, proposed by Horrigan et al. (1999), allocates joint production on the basis of the proportion of the time that a group spends on the solo activities. This method computes the total amount of time a demo-graphically defined group of people spend their time, on average, and assigns an hour of time spent by an individual jointly doing the activity on the basis of the proportion of the population totals. For example, if teenage girls spend 10 hours a week only on the phone and 20 hours a week only watching television, then 9 hours jointly spent talking on the phone while watching television would be allocated as 3 hours on the phone and 6 hours watching television. While this might be appropriate if one is aggregating time over multiplexed activities, participants pointed out that there is no justification for this divi-sion if the activities are truly simultaneous. It also is not appropriate if time spent jointly in two activities is different from the solo time spent in the two activities. In other words, the output of a half hour spent talking on the telephone while watching television may not be equivalent to the output of a half hour spent only talking on the phone, for example, if the quality of the conversation is lessened while multitasking. This approach would treat the two half hours the same.

A final approach, called the value theoretic measure of time use and described by William Nordhaus, divides time spent in joint activities by the value of the outputs produced by the time. For example, if a person is jointly cooking and babysitting and the value of babysitting is $5 per hour and the value of cooking is $15 per hour, then an hour of simultaneously babysitting and cooking would be allocated as 15 minutes of babysitting and 45 minutes of cooking. This approach would use either the value of the products for extrinsically valuable activities or the subjective value of the time for intrinsically valuable activities. This approach might be a useful framework for allocating simultaneous time use, particularly when integrated with the national income and product accounts. However, it poses serious practical obstacles because of the need to measure the outputs or values of alternative time uses.

Discussion at the workshop made it clear that finding a practical and theoretically satisfactory approach to measuring simultaneous activities is a tough issue. Existing surveys indicate that attention to simultaneous activities is important. Some activities, such as child care, often show up as secondary activities and would be lost if only primary activities are recorded and reported. Further research is needed on this issue. Whatever approach is taken, it is clearly important to allow for multiple activities in time-use surveys.

4

The Current State of Data on Time Use

The number of surveys that collect data on time use around the globe is growing, and some countries have made sustained commitments to collecting data on time use on a regular basis. Table 1, at the end of this chapter, summarizes major time-use studies around the world. Canada has just fielded its third time-use survey and will field one every 6 years. Australia conducted surveys of time use in 1992 and 1997 and will continue to do so every 5 years. The European Union's statistical agency, Eurostat, is conducting a large scale time-use survey that will collect data across 18 countries. In contrast, large surveys of time use in the United States have been fielded only four times in the past three decades.

To put these developments in context, this section describes time-use data collections that have been conducted in the United States and other countries. It also highlights some smaller, more targeted United States time-use studies that were mentioned during the workshop.

TIME-USE SURVEYS IN THE UNITED STATES

University of Michigan Surveys

In 1965-1966, the University of Michigan conducted a national time-use survey.[1] It was part of the Multi-National Time Budget Study (see Szalai et

---

[1] A national-level study of time use was conducted by the Bureau of Human Nutrition and Home Economics between 1924 and 1928 (see U.S. Department of Agriculture, 1944). Several

al., 1972), which included studies in 12 countries in North America and Western Europe. The Michigan Survey was limited to persons aged 18-64 and did not include those who lived in cities with fewer than 30,000 people or households without at least one member working at least 10 hours per week in the nonfarm sector of the economy. More than 1,200 people were in the sample. Interviews collected data on household demographic information; the status and characteristics of respondents' employment situation; ownership of land, vehicles, residence, and other consumer goods; and media usage and social-psychological measures. In addition, diaries were left with the sample members, to be filled out by respondents during the day after the interview. Respondents recorded the activities they were engaged in, the time the activities began and ended, whom they were with, where they were during the activity, and other activities engaged in simultaneously. The sample was designed so that the number of diaries collected on each day of the week would be equal across the week.[2]

The Institute for Social Research at the University of Michigan conducted two subsequent surveys of time use. The first was conducted in 1975 and 1976 (see Juster and Stafford, 1985 for details); the second was a follow-up with a subsample of the 1975-1976 sample, conducted in 1981 and 1982. Both studies used approximately the same design. In the first survey, 1,500 adults who were 18 and over (including those over the age of 64) and nearly 900 spouses were interviewed. Multiple interviews were conducted with each respondent over the year, approximately every three months to roughly cover the four seasons.

Unlike the 1965-1966 study, data for the 1975-1976 and 1981-1982 studies were collected through the use of a 24-hour recall diary, in which respondents were asked to record what they did the day before they were interviewed. Respondents were prompted to describe what they had done at one minute past midnight on the diary day. Interviewers also asked the respondent where they were during the activity, who was with them, and whether they were doing anything else at the same time. Then the interviewer asked the respondent what he or she did next and at what time the next activity began, and so on until all the time to midnight the next day was accounted for.

Over the four interviews in the year, data were collected for two weekdays, one Saturday, and one Sunday for each respondent and his or her spouse. The initial interview was conducted in person, and the next three were conducted over the phone. Some background information on respondents was

---

local and smaller scale time use-surveys were conducted prior to the Michigan study; see Bryant and Zick (1996b) for a summary.

[2]The same design was used in all participating countries.

collected for each of the four waves during the year, while other information was collected only for a single wave. The interviews collected basic demographic and household income data, as well as information on employment status and characteristics. Information was also collected on household organization (e.g., who does what tasks), technology and media usage, on the house or residence of the household, and household durables.

The 1981-1982 follow-up sampled almost half of the 1975-1976 sample members and their spouses. For each respondent, interviews were conducted on the same days of the week as in the previous survey. Again, four waves of interviews were given, approximately every three months. The format of the surveys in 1981-1982 were basically the same as in the 1975-1976 study: the only significant change was that proxy reports of time use for up to three of a respondent's children who were between the ages of 3 and 17 were also collected. The surveys also collected much of the same background data on the respondents and their spouses as the 1975-1976 study did. The 1981-1982 survey also collected data on the social supports available to respondents.

University of Maryland Surveys

In 1985, researchers at the University of Maryland conducted a large-scale national survey of time use, called the Americans' Use of Time Study (Robinson and Godbey, 1997; Robinson, 1999). Data from over 5,300 persons aged 12 and over were collected. This study also used an open-ended diary survey; however, the method for collecting the data was different from that of the Michigan studies. Random-digit dialing was used to screen households for a respondent at least 18 years or older. This person was then given a 2- to 5-minute orientation interview and was invited to participate in the mail-in diary study. If the person agreed, a diary was mailed to that person and to every member of his or her household who was aged 12 or over. These 1-day diaries specified the day to which they were supposed to refer and were to be filled out as the day proceeded. The survey also included a random-digit telephone survey of day-before activities (for those respondents initially contacted through the telephone sample) and a personal in-home interview for some respondents (as part of a separate sample).

The designated days for which the diaries were to be filled out were spread evenly across days of the week and throughout the calendar year. Data on primary activities and secondary activities were collected. Data on when the activity began and ended, who the respondent was with, and where the activity happened were also collected.

Since the 1985 study, U.S. cross-section time diary studies were conducted as part of this project in 1992-1994, 1995, and 1997-1998. All of these studies covered adults over the age of 18, and the 1992-1994 study included data for children.

TIME-USE SURVEYS IN OTHER COUNTRIES

Although many countries have collected and are collecting time-use data, Canada and Australia have made it a priority to regularly collect data on time use for their populations. Both studies were motivated primarily by a desire to measure unpaid work as input for satellite accounts to the national economic accounts.

Canadian Time-Use Surveys

Canada began collecting time-use data in 1986 and has fielded time-use surveys in 1992 and, most recently, in 1998 as part of a General Social Survey. Lorna Bailie from Statistics Canada reported on the 1998 survey during the workshop.

The 1998 survey collected data on 10,000 households for persons aged 15 and over. A computer-assisted telephone interview (CATI) survey was conducted, with the data collection period running from February 1998 to January 1999. Statistics Canada developed the CATI application of the time diary and introduced on-line coding of the activities during this round of the sur-. vey. Both techniques were successfully implemented with extensive monitoring to ensure high-quality results.

The 1998 survey also asked respondents, for the first time, "did this activity help a person outside your household or an organization?" for certain activities. If so, the respondent was further queried as to whether the person was 65 or older, her or his relationship to the respondent, and whether that person had a long-term health or physical limitation.

The survey included a retrospective diary for 24 hours and included questions about where the respondent was, whom the respondent was with, as well as the "for whom" component for certain activities. Data were collected only on primary activities (not secondary ones), but the information was supplemented with a child care diary that detailed when the child woke up and went to sleep and time spent looking after children. There was also a module on spouse's activities. The survey also included a series of stylized questions about unpaid work, education and learning, employment and working conditions, quality of life, cultural and sports activities, socioeconomic characteristics (such as income, place of birth, religion, language, perceived health status, sleep problems, and type of dwelling).

The survey was approximately 30 minutes long and of that, 10 minutes was spent responding to the diary. The interview began by obtaining a household roster, asking about everyone in the household—age, gender, and relationship. Respondents were allocated to a specific day of the week, and interviewers had 48 hours in which to complete the interview. Statistics Canada reported that the CATI was very helpful in editing and data quality control.

Because the interviewer was able to see the list of respondent reported activities, the amount of time spent for each and the list of individuals in the household, inconsistencies in reporting could be flagged and clarified as the interview was in progress.

Only one person in the household was interviewed, and only one diary was collected for each respondent. Prior to the main survey, Statistics Canada conducted a test in which two persons in the household were asked to complete a diary and two diaries for each person were collected. Nonresponse rates for this test were extremely high, and as a result, the traditional method of one person and one diary per household was subsequently used.

Australian Time-Use Surveys

The Australian survey was described as the "Mercedes of time-use surveys" by workshop discussant Lorna Bailie. This survey interviews all household members 15 years and older and collects time diary information over two days for each respondent. Two of these time-use surveys have been conducted, in 1992 and in 1997.[3] Each survey had a sample of approximately 7,000 people who completed diaries for two days of the week. Therefore, in total, a sample of 2,000 diaries were kept for each day of the week. The purpose of the surveys is to provide data to make estimates of the time that individuals spend in different activities for use in policy development and planning.

The 1997 Australian Time Use Survey information was obtained partly by interview and partly by self-completed diaries, which were left with the respondents to record their activities over the two days. One randomly selected member of each household was first interviewed to collect information on household composition, characteristics of individuals in the household aged 15 and older, and the use of technology and outsourcing of domestic tasks (for example, maid services or lawn mowing services). Diaries for each household member over the age of 15 were then left behind to be filled out and collected later. A paper-and-pencil diary was used to collect data for two consecutive days. The diary collected information on what the activity was, when it took place, where it took place, and with whom the activity took place. Data on simultaneous activities and care-giving activities were also collected. Both the 1992 and 1997 surveys included modules for child care activities and information on any disabilities of any people who were receiving care from the respondent.

---

[3]A dress rehearsal for the 1992 time-use survey was conducted in 1987; data from this dress rehearsal were also released.

Eurostat's Harmonized Time-Use Survey and Pilot Survey

Eurostat, the statistical agency for the European Community, has conducted a pilot time-use survey in 18 countries and is planning to conduct a full study that is harmonized across all countries (see Table 1 for the countries involved in the study). The objectives of the study are to improve national account estimates, better understand time use at work, better understand gender and family policy, understand common transport policy regarding passenger transport and tourism, and measure time use in leisure and cultural activities.

The pilot survey included household questionnaires, individual questionnaires, and time-use diaries. There were a core set of questions to be asked in all countries involved in the study. Individual countries added their own questions to this core.

All members of sampled households over the age of 10 were instructed to complete two diaries for two nonconsecutive days for each individual (one weekday and one weekend day). Time on the diaries was broken down into 10-minute slots, for which the individual described what he or she did. Questions covered secondary activities, who else was present, and who the respondent was helping if applicable. The 1996-1997 pilot study interviewed people in 3,400 households, with a total of 13,600 diaries. In conjunction with the larger Eurostat study, some countries are also conducting their own time-use studies. Italy will be collecting time-use diaries from 30,000 people, including children aged 3 and over. The Bulgarian study will collect diaries from 20,000 people, including infants and children.

OTHER TIME-USE SURVEYS

Each of the surveys described above are general purpose surveys aimed at obtaining nationally representative data for the population. Other time-use surveys have been targeted towards a particular population or group. A number of surveys have focused on the time use of children, to better understand child development, socialization, and well-being. Another study, conducted for the California Air Resources Board, was designed to determine the effect of second-hand smoke. Such studies sometimes ask only stylized questions about time use, such as how many minutes do you use the telephone each day, or how many times do you read to your child. Some have used both time diaries and stylized questions. Others have used the experiential sampling method of collecting data, in which respondents are given a beeper and are paged at random times during the day and asked to report what they are doing. This section describes some of these studies that were discussed at the workshop.

One of the larger time-use studies on children was recently conducted as a supplement to the Panel Study of Income Dynamics (PSID) at the University of Michigan, and was sponsored by the National Institute of Child Health and Human Development. The study targeted children aged 0-12 in 1995 PSID households. Time diaries over a 24-hour period for up to two children in each household were collected, usually from the child's primary care giver. Data for 3,600 children were collected. The interviews included some stylized questions and time diaries, which gave a chronological report about the child's activities over a specified 24-hour period. Diaries were collected for one weekday and one weekend day. Information on simultaneous activities was also collected. Sandra Hofferth reported some results of the study, specifically, on how the time diary data compare with data collected from stylized questions. These results are discussed in the following section. Several other targeted time-use studies for children and youth have been conducted (Almeida, 1997; Larson, 1989; Huston et al., 1997). In addition to children's time use, the PSID has also collected, on an on-going basis through stylized questions beginning in 1968, data on time spent doing housework.

An example of a more targeted time-use study is the 1987-1988 California Activity Pattern (CAP) Survey. This time-use diary study was funded by the California Air Resources Board to better understand time spent in daily activities "that had implications for air pollution exposure (presence of smokers, use of cooking equipment, use of solvents, etc.)" (Robinson et al., 1994: 3).

The CAP Survey is a probability random sample of 1,579 Californians aged 18 years and older in 1987-1988 who have telephones. A random-digit dialing survey was conducted. One eligible household member was randomly selected to be interviewed from each household. One 24-hour diary was collected from each sample member. The days of the week for which diaries were collected were spread throughout the week, with Sundays overrepresented. Diaries were also collected throughout the year except for the months of May and June. In addition to recording times spent in activities, data were collected on the locations of the activities and whether smokers were present during the activity. Interviews also collected general background information on respondents.

From data collected through a 24-hour time-use diary and through direct questions on smoking behavior, estimates of exposure to environmental tobacco smoke have been computed. Among other things, the data were used to estimate exposure to environmental tobacco smoke through the reports of activities, locations, and the presence of smokers.

TABLE 1 Major Time-Use Surveys

Country	Years	Sample Size	Response Rate (%)
Australia	1992	3,300 households yielding 12,000 diaries	69 (households); 83 (individuals)
	1997	*	72 (households); 84 of (individuals)
Bulgaria	1970-1971	*	*
	1976-1977	*	*
	1988	27,506 individuals in 9,150 households	98.4 (households)
Canada Halifax-Dartmouth Area	1971-72	2,141 individuals	*
National Pilot Study	1981	2,685 households subsampled from 1971 study	52
National Study	1986	12,500 households	80
	1992	12,765 households	77
	1998	* *	
Cuba	1967	* *	
Denmark	1975	* *	
EUROSTAT Harmonized Survey Finland, Greece, Ireland, Italy, Luxembourg, Portugal, Spain, Sweden, UK, Albania, Bulgaria, Hungary, Poland, Slovenia, Estonia, Latvia, Lithuania, FYROM	1996-1997	3,400 households yielding 13,600 diaries	60-65 over all countries
EUROSTAT Harmonized Survey France	Proposed 1998	*	*
EUROSTAT Harmonized Survey Finland, Italy, UK	Proposed 1999	*	*

Table continued on next page

TABLE 1 Continued

Country	Years	Sample Size	Response Rate (%)
Finland	1930, 1940s	Subsamples of school children and farm wives	*
	1967	Subsamples	*
	1969	Subsamples	*
	1971	Subsamples	*
	1975	Subsamples	*
	1979	Subsamples	*
	1987-1988	10,574 individuals	74.4
	1990	*	*
France	1986	*	*
Germany	1992	*	*
Great Britain	1974	*	*
	1980	Subsample of elderly	*
Hungary	1963	12,000 individuals from 12,000 households	*
	1976-1977	27,607 diaries	*
	1986-1987	8,297 diaries	*
Ivory Coast	1979	3,352 individuals	56
Japan	1960-1961	170,000 diaries	*
	1965	24, 000 diaries	*
	1976	* *	
	1980	68,000 diaries	*
	1986	* *	
	1991	* *	
	1996	99,000 households with 270,000 individuals	*
Latvia	1971	*	*
	1973	*	*
	1987	891 households	*
Lithuania	1974	*	*
	1988	984 employed individuals	*
The Netherlands	1986 pilot	*	*
	1987	6,668 individuals in 3,817 households	47
	1988	*	*

TABLE 1 Continued

Country	Years	Sample Size	Response Rate (%)
New Zealand	1990-1991 1998	* 8,500 individuals	* 70 and 66 for pilot
Norway	1971-1972 1980-1981	* 3,307 diaries	58 65
Poland	1975-1976	21,819 individuals	*
Sweden	1984-1985 pilot	2,000 individuals	63
Switzerland	1979-1980	*	*

Szalai International Study
  Belgium, Bulgaria,
  Czechoslovakia, France,
  Federal Republic of Germany,
  German Democratic Republic,
  Hungary, Peru, Poland, USA,
  USSR, and Yugoslavia
	1965-1966	778 - 2,891 individuals	Ranged from 60-100

USSR	1986	2,396 households	*
USSR	1924 1959-1965	* Roughly 100,000 diaries	*

NOTE: A number of these studies are old, and the results are not readily available in English. The empty cells denoted by * represent missing information about sample sizes and response rates.

SOURCE: Horrigan et al. (1999).

5

Survey Design Issues

The collection of time-use data presents many interesting survey design issues. Time-use studies may have the goal of not only sampling across the population, but also across hours of the day, days of the week, and seasons of the year. Surveys often have a goal of completely accounting for time use in a specified period, usually a day. For some studies, however, a sample of a day's activities may be sufficient to achieve the goals of the study. Often time-use studies need to collect information on where the respondent was during the activity, who the respondent was with, and whether the respondent was doing anything else in addition to the primary activity being reported. Some time-use studies also need to collect information on respondents' characteristics, how respondents felt during the activity, and other behaviors of the respondent.

One session of the workshop was devoted to discussing the various methods used to collect data on time use and survey design issues surrounding these methods. This session focused on two methods of collecting time-use data, the time diary method and the experiential sampling method. Participants also discussed how the quality of data and the feasibility of these methods compare with other methods of collecting time-use data, such as stylized questions on surveys (questions that ask respondents to estimate how much time they spend in certain activities) and observational approaches to measuring time use. This section first briefly describes each of these methods and then discusses some sampling and questionnaire content issues that relate to the methods.

METHODS FOR MEASURING TIME USE

Time Diary Method

The most widely used method for collecting time-use data for a large sample of persons is the time diary. This method was used for the four major time-use surveys in the United States, as well as for other large time-use surveys in the world (Australia, Canada, the 1965 Multi-national Time Use Survey, and the forthcoming Eurostat Harmonized Time Use Survey; see Table 1 in Chapter 4). The essence of the time diary method is that respondents are asked to make a complete record of their activities over a period of time, usually one day. Although it is not always the case, time diaries usually ask open-ended questions about the respondent's amount of time spent in activities. In other words, respondents enter the time an activity starts and finishes on a free-form basis, rather than in time slots of (say) 15 minutes. Activities are then typically classified and coded first into broad groups, and then into more specific groups according to a set standard. The first set of such coding standards were developed by Szalai for the Multi-National Time Budget Study. (Horrigan et al., 1999, summarize several different coding standards currently being used.)

Time diaries can be filled out during the day, or retrospectively. Sometimes, survey respondents are interviewed to orient the respondent to the survey, and then diaries are left behind with the respondent to be filled out for the next day. These are called leave-behind diaries, which were used in the University of Maryland and Australian time-use surveys. In contrast, a retrospective diary is one in which a respondent is asked to recall what he or she did for the "designated diary day"—the day for which the respondent has been asked to report his or her activities. Retrospective diaries were used in the 1975-1976 and 1981-1982 Michigan studies and the Canadian time-use studies.

The choice of a leave-behind diary or a retrospective diary has cost and data quality implications. Using leave-behind diaries tends to be more expensive because an orientation interview for the study must usually be given to the respondent prior to leaving the diary. An interview may also be needed after the diary is completed to clarify respondents' answers or to fill in missing information.[1] For retrospective diaries, respondents are oriented to the interview and provide responses in one setting or telephone call and so are less expensive. However, retrospective diaries rely on respondent's ability to recall how they spent their time, which may affect data quality (see below).

Although time diaries may be targeted to specific groups, they are readily

---

[1]This was a principal reason that the 1975-1976 Michigan study used a retrospective diary (Juster, 1999).

adaptable on a large scale. Typically, studies are conducted for a random sample of households. They are sometimes further randomized across days of the week, so that each randomly selected respondent is randomly assigned to a designated day or days to account for their activities. This method makes the entire sample of diaries representative across days of the week, which is important because there are likely systematic differences in time use across weekdays and weekend days. For leave-behind diaries, respondents are contacted and asked to fill out a diary for the next 24 hours. For retrospective diaries, respondents are often called or contacted one day and asked to recall what happened on the previous day, the designated day. Sometimes diaries are collected for several days for each respondent: a common method is to collect diaries for a weekday and a weekend day. Diaries are usually collected for only one household member who is randomly selected from all household members who are in the age range of the survey. The Australian studies collected time diaries from all members of the household over the age of 15; for other surveys, the expense of doing so usually limits the number of respondents.

In addition to collecting data on the activities and the time spans of the activities in which respondents engage, diaries may also collect information on whom the respondent was with, where the activity took place, and whether the respondent was doing anything else. The Canadian survey also asked whether the respondent was helping someone in or out of the household or helping an institution. Diaries might collect only very basic information about the respondent, such as age, race, and household size, or they may have extensive sets of questions on specific topics. As noted in Chapter 4, the 1998 Canadian time-use survey included questions on volunteer activities, educational activities, time spent in unpaid activities, and time spent in child care activities. Questions on how much time a respondent spent in a particular activity are called stylized questions. They are often used to supplement time diaries to gather information about activities that the regular diary may not capture (for example, another household member's time use or time spent being "on call" for child care—not actively caring for the child, but simply being present in case of an emergency—which may not be recorded as the primary activity for the time period and hence, may not be easily identified in diaries); that respondents are unwilling to report in a diary (sexual activity or drug use, for example); or for a longer reference period, since they may be unlikely to occur on the specified day. (Stylized questions are discussed further below.)

Recently, time-use diaries have been conducted over the telephone with Computer Assisted Telephone Interview (CATI) technology. The Canadian time-use survey used CATI. CATI is often less expensive than paper-and-pencil interviews. Using CATI can also help speed up interviews and allows validation of answers while an interview is ongoing (for example, interviewers may be notified when a value given by the respondent falls out of a valid range of answers), which can improve data quality. A problem in using CATI for time diaries is that interviewers are sometimes given considerable discretion to classify activities while the interview is in progress. Since different interviewers may classify similar activities differently, there may be variability in the classification of activities across interviewers. This means that special and careful attention to establishing coding procedures and to training interviewers about these procedures is needed.

The time diary method does have limitations. Most often, time diaries rely on respondent recall of activities, which is a potential source of error (see discussion below). Time diaries have also been found to underestimate activities with short time spans (see Juster, 1985), such as trips to the bathroom or going to the refrigerator for a snack.

Experiential Sampling Method

Another method for collecting data on how people spend time is called the experiential sampling method (ESM), which was primarily developed by Mihalyi Csikszentmihalyi and associates (see Csikszentmihalyi and Csikszentmihalyi, 1988; Csikszentmihalyi and Larson, 1992; and Zuzanek, 1999). ESM studies have typically been conducted to understand experiential, cognitive, and motivational aspects of activities, although these studies have also been used to estimate time spent in different activities.

The typical method used in ESM studies is to give survey respondents a pager, beeper, or programmable wrist watch that is randomly activated (beeped, vibrated or buzzed) throughout the day. When the respondent is beeped, he or she is asked to fill out a self-report of what he or she was doing and about various aspects of the activity. A respondent may be beeped many times within a day, and the study may cover a day, a week, or a month. The goal of these studies is to sample how people spend time, by randomly beeping them during the day and asking them to record what they are doing, who they are with, and how they feel during the activity, etc.

In general, the self-reports that respondents fill out include a core set of questions (Zuzanek, 1999): What day and time were you beeped? Where were you when you were beeped? Who were you with, what were you doing, and what were your thoughts at the time of the beep? Typically, these studies then ask questions about the respondent's experiential, motivational, and cognitive aspects of the activities. Box 1 shows a typical form that respondents are asked to fill out when they are beeped. Like time diaries, ESM studies allow respondents to specify the activity in which they are participating. This is in contrast to stylized questions about time use, which must prompt respondents about a particular activity (i.e., ask them how much time they spent doing a named activity instead of allowing respondents to name

Box 1   Typical Experiential Sampling Method Response Form

Date:___   Time Beeped: _____am/pm   Time Filled Out: _____

AS YOU WERE BEEPED:

What were you thinking about?_____
_____

Where were you? _____

What was the main thing you were doing?_____
_____

Who were you with?		
____ Spouse/Partner	____ Alone	
____ Your children	____ Friends/neighbors	
____ Other _____		

	Not at all	Somewhat	Quite	Very Much
How well were you concentrating?	____ ____	____ ____	____ ____	____ ____
Was it hard to concentrate?	____ ____	____ ____	____ ____	____ ____
Were you in control of the situation?	____ ____	____ ____	____ ____	____ ____
How pressed for time were you?	____ ____	____ ____	____ ____	____ ____

Describe how you felt as you were beeped (answer all):

	Very	Quite	Some-what	Neither/not sure	Some-what	Quite	Very	
Alert	____	____	____	____	____	____	____	Drowsy
Happy	____	____	____	____	____	____	____	Sad
Irritable	____	____	____	____	____	____	____	Cheerful
Energetic	____	____	____	____	____	____	____	Tired
Upset	____	____	____	____	____	____	____	Calm
Active	____	____	____	____	____	____	____	Passive
Worried	____	____	____	____	____	____	____	Carefree
Excited	____	____	____	____	____	____	____	Bored
Confused	____	____	____	____	____	____	____	Clear
Relaxed	____	____	____	____	____	____	____	Tense
Good	____	____	____	____	____	____	____	Bad

	0	1	2	3	4	5	6	7	8	9
Time was passing	——	—	—	—	—	—	—	—	—	——
	Slowly									Fast
Challenges of the activity:	——	—	—	—	—	—	—	—	—	——
	Low									High
Your skills, knowledge, or competence in the activity:	——	—	—	—	—	—	—	—	—	——
	Low									High
Do you wish you had been doing something else?	——	—	—	—	—	—	—	—	——	—
	Not at all								Very much	
How free were you to choose what you were doing?	——	—	—	—	—	—	—	—	——	—
	Not at all								Very much	
How interested were you in what you were doing?	——	—	—	—	—	—	—	—	——	—
	Not at all								Very much	

Did you do it
because:

___ You had to
___ You wanted to
___ There was nothing else to do
___ Other _____

Did you feel any of the following states as you were beeped?

	Not at all		Somewhat		Very much
Physical fatigue	——	——	——	——	——
Mental fatigue	——	——	——	——	——
Headache	——	——	——	——	——
Physical discomfort, stiffness, body aches	——	——	——	——	——

****

Great thoughts, wise cracks:

the activity themselves). This flexibility of reporting may make classifying activities more difficult. But it also means the data analyst can make his or her own classifications of activities for different purposes.

ESM surveys usually do not have the goal of completely accounting for an individual's time use. They are, rather, typically used to explore processes of daily behavior (Zuzanek, 1999). Consequently, they have advantages and limitations for measuring time use, depending on the purpose of the study. One advantage, relative to time diaries and stylized questions, is that since activities are recorded soon after the beeper signal is sent, recall error is not a concern. Responses may also be less susceptible to normative editing within the framework of the experiential sampling method because respondents are asked to immediately record what they were doing and have less time to construct an "acceptable" response. Furthermore, because the random beep method is more free form and respondents are often encouraged to express how they feel during the activity, respondents may feel less pressure to record only normatively sanctioned responses and, hence, may give more genuine responses.

Experiential sampling methods are useful in assessing human behavior and subjective emotional states and in understanding interpersonal relationships. An example of such a study is one where couples, who were both given beepers, were beeped at the same time (and sometimes in the same place) and asked to record their emotional states (Larson and Richards, 1994, as described in Zuzanek, 1999). The study uncovered a phenomenon of "unmutual togetherness;" even though couples were spending time together, they were emotionally not together. Finally, with longitudinal data, this method could be used to make causal links between emotional states.

There are limitations to experiential sampling time-use studies. First, they are more expensive than other methods, and therefore, may not be expandable to a large national survey. Second, as Jiri Zuzanek reported, while the response rates for beeps is good, typically, the studies are more burdensome on participants, and there may be a selection bias in that the people who agree to participate in the study are systematically different from the people who do not agree to participate. Gaining respondent compliance for larger representative samples is perhaps the biggest challenge facing these studies (Zuzanek, 1999). Another limitation is that they typically are not designed to fully account for all time in a day (or other time unit). ESM studies may also miss certain types of activities because respondents are not willing to carry the beeping, paging, or vibrating device with them while participating in certain activities because they do not want to interrupt what they are doing to fill out a survey. Juster and Stafford (1985) found that beeping respondents at random times recorded fewer activities outside of the home than time diary reports, presumably because respondents were less willing to carry the beeper device with them outside the home. However, as more and more people carry pagers and cellular telephones, this problem may be reduced.

Workshop participants were enthusiastic about the possibilities of the experiential sampling technique for certain purposive studies. Workshop participants suggested that it could be useful for health-related research, since emotions, feelings of pain or stress, and levels of exertion may be associated with activities. Participants also suggested that the method would be useful for understanding the time crunch or stress from the time crunch. Understanding the emotional states associated with different activities may also help classify activities by whether they give intrinsic or extrinsic rewards.

Several participants suggested that ESM could be extremely useful in uncovering how people spend their time at work. Time diaries are likely to be difficult to use in the context of work because they require a time commitment on the part of the respondent (if the respondent is filling out a diary as the day goes along). Further, if the goal of a study is to obtain detailed information on work activities (as opposed to broad categories of work activities) and if retrospective diaries are used, respondents may have difficulty recalling their activities because activities may be done for short intervals or because there may be interruptions so that the respondent must attend to another matter. For these reasons, obtaining a "sample" of the day's activities using the experiential sampling method or the random hour technique may be more appropriate. Either of these methods is likely to be a less burdensome method of collecting detailed data on time use at work than a method that completely accounts for all the time at work during the day. Both of them are less likely to be subject to normative editing of responses.

It was also suggested by workshop participants that experiential sampling studies could be used to cross-validate data produced from time diaries and stylized questions. A similar technique–the random-hour technique–has been used in the past to cross-validate data: time diary respondents are called randomly on the day they are filling out their diaries to cross-validate responses for the given hour (see Robinson, 1999). While the experiential sampling method is unlikely to be the primary method of collecting data for a national study of time use, participants said that further work towards integrating time diaries with such studies would be beneficial for understanding time use.

Stylized Questions

Stylized questions are another method to measure time use, asking respondents how much time they spend in certain activities. Some examples are: About how much time do you spend cooking in your home during the week? About how much time do you spend caring for you child on a daily basis? Questions can be open-ended, where respondents can fill in a number of hours, or they can have a range of answers, where respondents choose one answer from categories such as "never," "once a week," "several times a week," or "every day." Many surveys with goals other than measuring time use have used these types of questions, usually as indicators of behavior patterns. For example, a health survey may ask how many times a respondent exercises each week. A survey with the purpose of measuring child development may ask how often a parent reads to a toddler.

Although stylized questions have the advantage of being the least expensive way to measure how people use their time, using this method as a way to estimate time spent in activities across the population is troublesome, mainly because the answers that respondents give have a high degree of error in them: that is, respondents underreport or overreport time spent in different activities. There are several reasons that stylized questions are prone to error. First, people may overreport activities that are socially "good" activities. For example, Sandra Hofferth reported on comparisons of stylized measures of time spent reading to children to time diary reports of time spent reading to children; she concluded that parents exaggerate the amount of time they spend reading to their children through stylized measures relative to the amount of time reported in a time diary. John Robinson also described a study in which stylized reports of church-going were much higher than time spent at church as measured by diary data. Similarly, respondents may underreport socially "bad" activities, such as time spent watching television.

Another reason that stylized questions may be measured with error is because respondents have a difficult time recalling what they have done over the time period the question references, if the question asks how much time the respondent spent doing a certain activity over the past week (or day or month or year). Respondents may also have a difficult time recalling and conceptualizing what a "typical" or "average" week is like in responding to such questions about time use in the activity over the week. For activities that take place on a daily basis, such as time spent commuting to work, the respondent may be able to make a much better estimate of the average time spent in the activity over the week. However, for activities that take place on a more variable basis, such as time spent talking on the phone, respondents may have a more difficult time recalling the amount of time spent in the activity. (These recall issues are discussed further below.)

Third, stylized measures of time use do not take into account any activities that occur simultaneously. This may be important for measuring passive activities, like watching television. The television may be turned on for many hours a day, but respondents may be doing many other things while the television is on. When asked how many hours of television were watched each day, respondents may not know whether to report the time spent solely watching the television screen or the total time they spent passively "watching" television while doing other activities. Depending on whether the respondent judges time spent passively watching television as an activity worth reporting, the amount of time spent watching television may be over- or underreported.

Another disadvantage to stylized questions is that the questions must be worded so that the respondent understands the types of activities for which the respondent is to report time use. That means that the activities need to be defined and classified within the question; in contrast, in a time diary, the activities are coded after the respondent has completed the diary.

Despite the problems with stylized questions, workshop participants agreed that there is a role for this method. Stylized questions can effectively be used to measure incidence of certain activities, especially those activities that occur infrequently, such as how much time was spent on vacations or how many days were spent in the hospital over the past year. Some workshop participants suggested that stylized questions are better for a specific and short time period (such as whether the respondent did a particular activity *yesterday*) than questions about usual activities over a day or week (such as whether the respondent usually does a particular activity on a weekly or daily basis). Cognitive testing of survey questions that ask for stylized reporting of time spent in activities can enhance the abilities of these types of questions to obtain valid measures of time use. Some previous research shows that some stylized questions are not measured with as much error as others (e.g., time spent at work, traveling, and shopping [Juster and Stafford, 1985]). As Francisco Samaniego suggested, well-designed stylized questions could be selectively used to obtain very specific information. Well-designed stylized questions cannot substitute for a complete account of time spent in all activities, but, they may be suitable for counting the time spent in a very specific activity.

Observational Approaches

On some occasions, direct observation of an individual's daily activities may be possible. In observational studies, an "interviewer" records what the respondent does during the day as opposed to the self-reports used in diaries, ESM studies, and stylized questions. For example, anthropologists have long used this approach in studying different cultures, and some child development studies use cameras or observational rooms to record how children spend their time in a controlled setting. John Robinson reported that he has recently trained students to "shadow" people they know throughout a day and record their activities, which are later validated against the trackee's own diary report of activities for the day. Use of electronic tracking devices might also be included in the category of observational studies. Robinson (1999) gives the example of media rating services that use electronic badges to record when the participants are near operating televisions or radios as a way of understanding time spent watching television.

The key advantage of observational studies is that they are very accurate. Their biggest drawbacks are that they are intrusive, may contain little useful information, and are expensive. Furthermore, since consent is usually needed from participants, participants know that they are being watched which means that they may change their behavior for the camera or the observer. However, in some settings, observational studies can be very useful, both in their own right and as a way to validate data collected through other means. For example, given parental consent, observational studies of children in day care settings or even school settings may provide a good source of data for studying child development.

Workshop participants were very supportive of the use of multiple methods in a single study. As Norman Bradburn noted, the advantages and limitations of each method are known. Further understanding of how these methods can be used in tandem to get to the information that is needed would be valuable in understanding time use. For example, it will be useful to know which stylized questions can be used in conjunction with diary studies to save survey costs. Or, a single study may find it useful to measure some activities through experiential sampling and others through a time diary. Understanding the methodological underpinnings of using these methods in tandem is an important area for future research. In addition, if certain methods are known to produce biases in reporting, research could be conducted to assess the extent of the bias. If the bias can be determined, then less expensive methods of collecting data can be used, despite their biases, because adjustments can be made to correct the bias.

SAMPLING ISSUES

Respondent Recall in Diary Surveys

One problem with retrospective diary studies is that respondents are asked to recall what they did, usually over the past 24 hours, but respondents may not be able to recall accurately what they have done. This measurement problem also relates to sampling issues for diary studies in which, it is common to obtain diaries across all the days of the week. It is important to sample across days of the week because time use is likely to be different for weekends and weekdays, and perhaps even between weekdays, (Mondays and Fridays may not be the same as Tuesdays, Wednesdays, and Thursdays). Typically, once a household is randomly chosen for the sample, it is then randomly assigned to provide a diary for a day of the week (or a random weekday and weekend day). Using this "designated" day method has implications for recall error, because it is often difficult to contact a respondent soon after the respondent's designated day. At issue is how long after the designated day respondents can be contacted and expected to provide high-quality recalls of their activities for the designated day. Should respondents who are not contacted the day after be contacted two or more days after (and still report on the designated day), or should they be counted as nonresponders, or, perhaps should they be contacted the following week on the same day of the week?

There has been some research on this topic. In her discussion of the Statistics Canada survey, Lorna Bailie explained that it allows for a 48-hour recall period without significant deterioration of data quality. In contrast, Juster and Stafford (1985) found that recall error rates increased if the recall period for a designated day that was a weekday was more than 24 hours (e.g., if a respondent was contacted on Wednesday or later and asked to recall what happened on the preceding Monday). However, this study also found that the recall period for weekend designated days could be extended for up to a week with little increase in error rates. Echoing Juster and Stafford's findings, Norman Bradburn cautioned against more than a 24-hour recall, as memory deterioration speeds up after that, especially for weekdays.

Workshop participants discussed some ways that recall error could be reduced. Using CATI methods is one way, where cross-validation of answers can take place as respondents can be asked to clarify their answers, if needed, during the interview. With further developments in cognitive research in surveys, questions could be better designed to enhance respondent recall. Participants also suggested that with longitudinal surveys, where diaries are kept for each respondent more than once, respondents become better at recalling their activities as they fill out more diaries and become familiar with the diary processes.

Data on Multiple Days of the Week for Each Observation

Individuals' time allocations to different activities can vary greatly across the days of the week and across seasons of the year. The activities that occur on weekdays are likely to be quite different than the activities that occur on weekend days. Furthermore, a one-day diary might represent an atypical day for the respondent. Over a large national sample where days of the week are equally represented (or if there is a controlled sample of days), this may not be as great an issue, because any atypical days would wash out in the aggregate. However, in using microdata for examining individual behavior, it may be crucial to obtain accounts of time use for multiple days for each individual. The ESM technique typically collects data for each day of the week for each respondent in the sample. Variation in time use across different days of the week could be captured using this method. Time diaries are typically not collected for every day of the week, although previous time diary surveys have collected data for a couple of days of the week for each respondent. The 1975-1976 and 1981-1982 Michigan time diary studies collected data on four different days of the week for each sample member (over the course of a year). The Australian surveys collected diaries on two con-secutive days for each respondent.

Collecting multiple diaries from each sample member may increase the cost of a survey, and it may have implications for response rates. Respondents may be reluctant to agree to participate in a diary study if they are expected to fill out more than one diary. In a methodological test conducted in conjunc-tion with the Canadian time-use survey, adults in single-person household who were asked to complete diaries for two days had an 88 percent response rate, but married couples' response rates (where both spouses were asked to fill out diaries for two days) were only 46 percent.

Having multiple diaries from each respondent can reduce sampling error and can be done in a cost-effective manner. As noted above, some evidence indicates that recall for time use on a weekend deteriorates at a slower rate than for weekdays. If a study collects a weekday and weekend day diary for each respondent, it may be possible to get diaries for both days during one interview, a day after the designated weekday. For example, a respondent with designated days of Saturday and Tuesday would be interviewed on Wednesday, the day after the designated weekday. This method may be more cost-efficient and also less harmful to response rates if both diaries can be completed during one, instead of two, telephone calls.

Data on Multiple Household Members

Another sampling issue raised at the workshop was whether diaries should be collected from more than one person in a household. From a conceptual standpoint, one argument for collecting time diaries from multiple persons in a household is to better understand labor force participation of household members, intrahousehold resource and time allocation, and who delivers fam-ily care (for children or other relatives). Child development researchers may also be interested in time use by children and adults in a household. In the public policy arena, it is also useful to have time diaries for multiple persons: for example, to understand the effects of a tax credit for households that provide care for elderly relatives, it is important to have data on the time use of all household members who could be providing the care.

Collecting diaries for multiple persons within a household may be diffi-cult because interviewing more than one member of the household means that the interviews will take longer. Statistics Canada believed that this was one reason for the low response rate in the test study where diaries were obtained from multiple household members of the Canadian time-use sur-vey. It may also be difficult to find a time to interview each household mem-ber who is part of the study. If one household member is interviewed, but other household members are not available for interview, the question arises about which day the second household member should be interviewed. Again, recall is a key issue. If a wife is interviewed on a Wednesday about her Tuesday activities, but the husband is not available for an interview on Wednesday, should the husband be interviewed on Thursday for Tuesday's activities (with some recall error) or for Wednesday's activities (which means activities for husbands and wives are recorded for different days)?

Many workshop participants agreed that there are some tricky issues to resolve in collecting diaries for multiple household members. However, the availability of data on multiple persons would greatly enhance the value of such data for understanding household behavior. Furthermore, as Juster (1999) argues, there are benefits for minimizing sampling error and statistical noise to collecting information on multiple household members and at multiple times for each household member (see also Kalton, 1985). Many workshop participants argued that data on multiple household members should be collected.

MATCHING DATA COLLECTION TO DATA USE

In choosing a method for measuring time use, the analytical purpose of the study should be the guiding principle (Bittman, 1999). While time diaries are probably the best method for collecting data on time use on a large scale, most workshop participants agreed that the other methods clearly have roles to play in collecting time-use data. For example, time diaries and stylized questions often do not provide much detail on respondents' use of time while at work. ESM studies could be useful in such a setting, however, as they are less subject to normative editing, require less time by respondents than do time diaries, and can be relatively easily adapted to diverse work settings. For other situations, it may be possible to use stylized questions to measure some activities, for example, to measure events that happen quite infrequently, making them more easily recalled by respondents, such as time spent on family vacations.

Which covariates are collected with time-use measures—that is, the supplementary information about respondents and their behavior—should also be guided by the uses of the data. For example, to assess subjective well-being during activities, an experiential sampling study may need to collect data on a person's emotional state and surroundings. To understand household labor force participation decisions, it is important to have data on wages, past work experience, and income of household members. If the goal of a time-use survey is to better understand household production, then data are needed on the technology and capital stock available to the household, as well as on inputs to the household production process.

It is likely that no single survey is going to be able to collect all the covariates that researchers will want or need. Therefore, a time-use survey may need to be linked to other data sets with a wider range of covariates or modules to the survey could be added as needed. Workshop participants emphasized the need to carefully consider which covariates are collected and how they are collected in developing a time-use survey.

THE 24-HOUR CONSTRAINT AND STYLIZED QUESTIONS

As has been noted by Robinson (1985) and others, data collected in stylized time-use surveys often violate the 24 hours per day (or 168 hours per week) constraint. There are several suggested ways of dealing with this effect. For example, in the pilot BLS time-use survey carried out by Westat in 1997, the working rule of shrinking reported time toward the constraint was advocated: the recommended strategy would shrink 30 reported hours in a given day to 24 by proportional shrinkage for all reported categories (from 10 hours of sleep to 8, for instance). It appears that approaches to the treatment of such data are largely ad hoc, and there is considerable room for additional research on this issue and for more comprehensive guidance on the analysis of such data. Some ways of dealing with the 24-hour problem are covered in Chapter 3 (Conceptual Issues) under "Simultaneous Activities." Other ways are discussed here.

In considering a simplified version of a (stylized) time-use survey in which each respondent reports the number of hours spent on two mutually exclusive and exhaustive categories (e.g., work and nonwork), the number of hours of each activity reported in a day should clearly total 24. However, there might be a number a perfectly plausible reasons why the number of hours do not add to 24, most likely because some simultaneous activities (e.g., time spent grading papers while providing child care) are counted twice. It is also possible that the tally in each category is done with relative independence and that the separate reports simply do not obey the constraint.

In his presentation at the workshop, Samaniego illustrated modeling these data as observations from a mixture of two bivariate normal distributions, pointing out that there may well be two types of respondents—those who obey the constraint and those who do not. He derived the maximum likelihood estimate of the bivariate mean. This exercise was devised to demonstrate that the "right approach" to estimating the mean time spent in each of the two activities depends crucially on the model assumed to govern the available data. In a particular example, Samaniego demonstrated that the maximum likelihood approach led to a markedly different prescription for estimating mean time use than the "shrink toward the constraint" strategy advocated in other studies. Samaniego suggested that the modeling of time-use survey data merited more research and greater care and that mathematical statistics might be usefully brought to bear on some on the thorny questions posed by the constrained estimation problems that often accompany such surveys.

6

The Proposed BLS Time-Use Survey

T he last national level survey of time use in the United States was fielded nearly 15 years ago, but the Bureau of Labor Statistics now has a well-developed plan to conduct a national-level survey of time use. During the workshop, representatives from BLS presented a report on the feasibility of the survey (Horrigan et al., 1999). In this section we review the history of the BLS efforts, describe the proposed survey, and summarize the workshop discussion of the proposal.

HISTORY

The Unremunerated Work Act of 1993 included a directive for the BLS to conduct a time-use survey for the purpose of counting unremunerated work performed in the United States and to calculate the monetary value of that work.[1] Since the act was introduced, the BLS has developed and tested a pilot time-use survey, cosponsored a conference, established a working group for exploring the feasibility of a time-use survey, and developed the report presented at this workshop.

The pilot study was conducted during 1997 under a contract with Westat. The first phase of the study included 21 cognitive interviews designed to understand respondents' difficulties in recalling activities from the past day. During the summer of 1997, a test random-digit dial telephone survey with

---

[1]This proposed law was not enacted.

1,000 interviews was fielded. Two types of interviews were conducted, with 500 interviews in each. The first asked respondents to recall what they were doing when, where they were doing it, and who was with them at the time. The second, aimed at measuring simultaneous activities, asked respondents what they were doing and whether they were doing anything else at the same time. Results of the test showed that some activities were underreported when respondents were not given the opportunity to distinguish simultaneous activities in the survey (primary and secondary activities). More time in nonmarket work activities was reported through the second type of interview, where respondents were cued to count time spent in simultaneous activities (Horrigan et al., 1999).

In the fall of 1997, the BLS cosponsored a conference with the MacArthur Network on Family and the Economy called "Time Use, Nonmarket Work and Family Well-Being." The conference brought together experts from a range of social science fields to talk about the economic aspects of time use, time use for children and families, childhood development and time use, public policy and time use, and methodologies for collecting time use data. Following the conference, the commissioner of BLS established a working group to examine the feasibility of collecting time-use data. The working group began with the following assumptions (Horrigan et al., 1999):

(1) The purpose of the survey would be to estimate the time individuals spend in various activities.

(2) The sample for the survey would be drawn from the outgoing rotation groups of the monthly Current Population Survey.

(3) A 24-hour day time diary would be used.

(4) The data collection protocol would be a computer assisted telephone interview (CATI).

The report and recommendations of the working group were presented at the workshop by the group's chair, Michael Horrigan.

CURRENT PLANS

The proposed time-use survey will draw a sample that is designed to be representative of the U.S. population 16 years of age and older. The survey will be designed to produce quarterly estimates of the proportion of time spent in different activities for this population and separately for a set of comparison groups. There are seven proposed sample stratification variables: gender; the presence of children (any under 6, any between 6-17, none under 18); education (less than high school, high school, some college, college graduate with no additional schooling, post-college study); age (16-24, 25-54, 55-64, 65 and older); employment (employed, unemployed, out of the labor force); family type (married couple families, families maintained by single adults, adults not in families); location (urban or rural); and race/ethnicity (Hispanic, non-Hispanic black, other). The survey will also be designed to generate annual estimates of a wide range of activities for an average week, weekday, and weekend day. Appendix C contains the classification codes of activities for which estimates will be produced. The proposed classification system is a modified version of the Australian system and is comparable to international coding systems.

A subsample of the Current Population Survey (CPS, a monthly survey conducted by the Census Bureau) would be used for the survey. A subsample of persons aged 16 and over who were in responding households will be drawn from the outgoing panels of the CPS.[2] The CPS interviews about 150,000 individuals in approximately 72,000 households each year. Given that one member of each CPS responding household is eligible for the proposed time-use survey and given nonresponse over the course of the CPS, the maximum possible sample size for the time-use survey is 72,000 per year. However, because the CPS oversamples small states and the goal of the time-use survey is not to be state representative but, rather, nationally representative, the maximum available sample size is closer to 54,000 per year. A subsample of these 54,000 will be drawn for the time-use survey. Currently, the proposal calls for at least 20,000 adults to be contacted annually. The proposal also calls for an additional 14,000 to be included in the sample to target smaller demographic populations (based on the stratification groups), for a total of 34,000 in the sample yearly. Assuming a response rate of 70 percent, the projected sample size will be about 24,000.

The proposed strategy to gather information on an individual's time use is to use the designated day approach: each household in the survey will be assigned a day of the week for which the respondent will report his or her activities. An attempt to interview the respondent will be made the day after the designated day. If the respondent cannot be reached the day after his or her designated day, the respondent will be reassigned the same day of the week for the next week. In other words, if a person with a designated day of Monday cannot be reached the Tuesday immediately following the designated day, that person will be reassigned to the next Monday and another attempt will be made to contact him or her following the next Monday. Up to four attempts to contact the individual will be made. Concern about recall error resulted in this approach. It was decided that relying on a recall period

---

[2]The CPS uses a rotating panel design: panels of individuals are interviewed monthly for 4 months, are not interviewed for the next 8 months, and are then interviewed again for the next 4 months. Every month a new panel begins the 16-month rotation. Those finishing their eighth month of interviewing will be eligible for the time-use survey subsample.

of more than 24 hours would diminish the quality of the data too much, but that nonresponse would be too high without reassignment. The assignment of individuals to days will be made so that half the days for which data are reported will be weekdays and half the days will be weekend days. Ten percent of the sample members will be assigned to each weekday (Monday through Friday), 25 percent will be assigned to Saturday and 25 percent will be assigned to Sunday.

The feasibility report also recommends that data be collected on a monthly basis and reported on a quarterly basis, to cut across all seasons of the year. As currently proposed, data will not be collected for holidays (individuals will not be assigned to a designated day that is a holiday).

The survey instrument will be composed mainly of an activity questionnaire (the time-use diary), which will document activities by the sample member over a 24-hour period. The survey will use CATI and respondents will be asked to recall the timing of their activities sequentially. Respondents will also be asked where they were during the activity, whom they were with, and whether they were doing anything else at the same time in order to record simultaneous activities. Respondents will also be asked what activities were done for pay to be able to better identify market and nonmarket activities. See Appendix D for the draft questionnaire presented at the workshop. The current proposal calls for time spent in simultaneous activities to be divided up according to the proportion of time members of the individual's demographic group spend on the two activities in solo (see Chapter 3).

In addition to the time-use component of the survey, other data on respondents will likely be collected. Those data include updated (from the CPS) household composition information, updated total family income, the respondent's labor force status, the labor force status of his or her spouse or partner, updated earnings information for the respondent, and school enrollment. The projected length of interview is approximately 25 minutes; completing the diaries is estimated to take approximately 22 minutes of the total. The estimate is based on the pilot test results for the time-use component and on experience with the CPS for update information.

In addition to the quarterly and annual estimates of time spent in various activities, the data could also be used to produce information on time spent in simultaneous activities and various estimates of time spent in activities around a theme, such as child care activities. These thematic estimates would add together time spent in the activity solely and simultaneously. The proposal calls for a public-use database to be made available for the research community.

Because the sample members for the proposed time-use survey are also CPS sample members, the new data could be linked to the various CPS supplements. The BLS working group also considered several topical modules that could be attached to the time-use survey, such as: use of tools, child care, elder or adult care, working hours, division of labor within the household, household production, volunteer activities, subjective assessments of activities, and subjective questions about the experience of time.

DISCUSSION

Workshop participants were generally very enthusiastic about the proposed time-use survey, but there were some concerns about the topics covered in the survey and the methodologies proposed.

One concern, raised by Nancy Folbre, regarded the measurement of time spent in child care activities. She was concerned that the core questions of the proposed survey are not refined enough to distinguish the time parents spend in direct interaction with children in contrast to the time spent in indirect care for children (such as being "on call"). The distinction is important for determining how labor force participation, wages, and public policies affect the allocation of time spent in direct child care activities and how qualitative aspects of time spent with children relate to outcomes. Jeanne Brooks-Gunn also expressed this concern.

Other participants were concerned about accurately measuring time spent in the labor force and in educational activities because detailed information about what the respondent does during these times may be difficult to obtain with a time diary. Several participants argued it would also be useful to collect information about the flexibility of work hours from survey respondents. People with flexible schedules may use their time differently, for example, by commuting during non-rush hour times. The rigidity of one's work schedule may also have implications for one's availability to provide care for a child, elder relative, or a relative who is ill. No survey can include all the topics that interest researchers, policy makers, and the public because survey resources are limited. In making decisions about topics covered, workshop participants encouraged the BLS to set priorities for data collection. In doing so, the participants stressed the need for the data collection to be guided by how the data will be used. They did note that using outgoing CPS panels as the sample frame means that there are opportunities to link time-use data to previously collected CPS data and that it may be possible to add topical modules later as needed.

Workshop participants were also enthusiastic about the survey because it will provide an excellent opportunity to test and develop alternative methods of collecting time-use data. Many participants emphasized the need to know how alternative approaches to collecting time-use data can be used together to gain a comprehensive picture of time use. For example, Thomas Juster suggested that a random hour technique could be used to collect data on time use in a work setting since this method is less burdensome on a respondent's time than a time diary. Lorna Bailie explained that the Canadian time-use survey used stylized questions about the time use of the respondent's spouse to substitute for not having the resources to interview more than one member of the household. Norman Bradburn urged BLS to conduct a systematic methodological program in conjunction with the main survey. Such a program could test different methodologies for collecting the data so that future data collection capacity could be built. Several participants urged that experts from a broad range of fields be consulted in the development of the tests. For example, Nancy Folbre suggested using ethnographers to get more detailed information on how people use time, and that studies using the experiential sampling method could further enhance knowledge of subjective measures of time use. Norman Bradburn suggested that cognitive psychologists could be consulted to develop stylized questions and to develop techniques for enhancing respondent recall for diaries. Several workshop participants suggested that a mechanism to give researchers and data users early input and advice for the BLS on questionnaire content and survey design be established.

As currently planned, the BLS survey will collect diaries from only one household member. Many workshop participants stressed the importance and usefulness of collecting diaries for multiple household members. Daniel Hamermesh emphasized the need for time-use data for husbands and wives, highlighting many of the conceptual and public policy issues (summarized in Chapter 3) for which such data would be useful. Collecting time-use diaries from multiple household members will lengthen the survey, and sample members may be less willing to respond if the interview is too long. However, workshop participants suggested that a well-developed survey that is interesting to the respondents and properly trained interviewers will help ensure that high-quality data are collected with a longer survey. In terms of who in the household is interviewed, many participants urged the BLS to include those between the ages of 11 and 16 in the sample to provide valuable data on adolescents.

Another methodological issue of concern was how days of the week would be sampled. As noted above, current plans call for each weekday to be sampled evenly (10 percent for each day) and for Saturday and Sunday to be sampled at 25 percent each. Daniel Hamermesh and Mihalyi Csikszentmihalyi both reported on research that showed that time-use patterns on Mondays and Fridays are different from time use patterns on Tuesdays, Wednesdays and Thursdays. Consequently, they argued that Mondays and Fridays should not be treated the same as other weekdays: consideration should be given to designating more than 10 percent of the sample to Monday and more than 10 percent to Friday. Oversampling these two days, in comparison with each day in the middle of the week (Tuesday-Thursday), would be beneficial to understanding what happens outside of the workplace because Mondays and Fridays tend to be atypical workdays. Several workshop participants also suggested that holidays should be included in the sample of designated days.

Some workshop participants also expressed concern over the plan to re-assign designated days to the same day the following week. The concern is that sample members who cannot be reached on the day after the designated day may always be unreachable on that day of the week. Also of concern is that data will not be collected on the days that respondents cannot be reached, which may be different days in terms of work schedules, travel schedules, etc. Yet it may be useful to document time spent in various activities during these unusual days. An alternative methodology suggested was to keep the same designated day, but allow for a longer recall period and try to reach the re-spondent later in the week. As discussed above, there are measurement error implications for using this methodology.

Collecting multiple diaries from the same person at different times and over different times of the year was also stressed as important considerations for the proposed survey. Some workshop participants argued for longitudinal time-use data to better understand changes in behavior in response to either policy changes or changes in family circumstances that cross-sectional data cannot provide. Participants also argued that collecting longitudinal data on sample members could help capture fluctuations in time use over different times of the year, which may be important for studying specific populations, such as school-aged children and their families or employees with seasonal variations in work schedules, or for studying specific activities, such as vaca-tion travel or outdoor recreation.

Despite the methodological issues raised in the discussion of the BLS proposal, it was evident from the discussion that participants considered the BLS survey to have a sound beginning and that it should move forward. Overall, workshop participants were enthusiastic about the potential for a large national survey on time use. Though the methodological concerns pro-vide challenges, participants suggested that these concerns are not serious enough to affect development of the survey. Robert Michael emphasized that statistics on time use have been missing from the federal statistical package for far too long and that data collected through the proposed BLS survey will be a significant step in furthering understanding of human behavior and social policy.

7

Summary

From the paper presentations and discussions during the workshop, several overarching themes emerged. This section summarizes these common themes, lacing together key threads of discussions from each of the workshop sessions.

IMPORTANCE OF U.S. TIME-USE DATA

Data on time use are important sources of information, and the lack of national time-use data is a critical gap in the federal statistical system. Time-use data produced on a regular and on-going basis can advance knowledge of the well-being of the U.S. population and can be used to inform public policy. Some examples of how time-use data can be used that were discussed in detail at the workshop include: better measures of labor inputs for productivity statistics; improvements in the coverage of national income and product accounts; understanding the changing nature of child care and elder care; understanding the effects of welfare reform; additional understanding of the role of retired persons in the nation; and better understanding of the "time crunch" felt by many people.

Time-use data can also be used to further understanding of household behavior, including the allocation of time and goods among household members and subjective feelings and satisfaction levels associated with time spent in different activities. Time-use data are also important for making international comparisons. Improved coverage in national income and product accounts that include measures of nonmarket production can enhance our knowledge of differences in output across countries and improve our ability to compare the output and income of the United States with those of other high-income countries and countries with developing economies. Time-use data can also be used to help understand cultural and social differences across countries.

Efforts to collect data on time use in other countries are more advanced than those in the United States. Australia and Canada both have regular and comprehensive surveys for collecting time-use data on a national basis. A harmonized European time-use survey that will be conducted in almost 20 countries is also moving forward through Eurostat. The United States does not currently collect regular and comprehensive time-use data on the American population.

PROPOSED BLS TIME-USE SURVEY

The Bureau of Labor Statistics has issued a report on the feasibility of conducting a time-use survey of the U.S. population. The report proposes to collect time diaries from a sample of the adult population of the United States from members of the outgoing rotation of the Current Population Survey. Overall, workshop participants acknowledged the need for and value of a national time-use survey and greeted the prospect of a future BLS time-use survey with enthusiasm. The proposed time-use survey can go a long way towards furthering understanding of many of the policy and behavioral issues discussed in this summary. A common theme emerging from the workshop discussion is that the BLS proposal is, on the whole, timely and carefully designed and ready to be taken to the next stage of development and refinement as a prelude to full deployment.

Economic and Demographic Characteristics

A number of design features of time-use surveys were highlighted at the workshop. To achieve a better understanding of household time allocation, nonmarket household production, and the effects of public policy on time use, many workshop participants emphasized the importance of collecting the fullest possible array of individual and household-level economic and demographic variables as possible. Such variables include, but are by no means limited to, age, race, gender, household structure and size, age and number of children, education levels of household members, income and wealth, labor force status, occupation, and wage rates. The CPS already collects data on many of these characteristics and the proposed BLS time-use survey plans to update these data. In addition to the regular CPS-collected data, workshop participants stressed the importance of collecting the widest possible array of background characteristics. Collecting the broadest array of covariates as possible is especially important for research uses of the data. The range of topics that can be researched with the data will expand as the range of covariates collected expands.

Multiple Diaries from the Same Respondent

Time use by a household can vary greatly from day to day and from season to season, because of work schedules, schooling schedules for households with children or educators, or simply because of atypical events that occur from time to time. Because of variation across days of the week, many workshop participants urged the BLS to collect data for multiple days of the week for each respondent to better capture the variability in time use across different days of the week.

Workshop participants also discussed the significant benefits of collecting longitudinal time-use diaries, that is, collecting diaries from each respondent at different times of the year. Longitudinal diaries could be collected to understand variation in time-use activities across seasons and they can be used to assist researchers in modeling changes in time-use behavior between two points in time. For example, if a person becomes employed between the two dates for which the time diaries are collected, one could examine changes in time allocated to nonmarket household production and to leisure activities for people who experience such a change in employment.

Interviewing respondents multiple times however, does present survey design and cost considerations, especially since the outgoing panel of the CPS, which is comprised of respondents who have already been through several rounds of surveys, will be used to develop the time-use sample. Careful consideration of such design issues will need to be made. There are precedents in collecting multiple diaries from survey respondents, from which lessons can be drawn: the Michigan studies collected diaries at four different times over the course of the year and Australia's studies collect data for two consecutive days from each sample member.

Diaries from Multiple Household Members

Many policy and behavioral questions about household time use involve the interaction of time use among family members. For example, if a wife receives a wage increase, the husband's time spent in market and nonmarket activities may change since the relative price of the husband's time to the wife's time has now decreased. Another interesting question is how the Earned Income Tax Credit affects both husbands' and wives' time spent in market work. Interactions between children's time use and parents' time use are similarly important in understanding household behavior. To address these questions, data for multiple members of a household would need to be collected. Workshop participants acknowledged that there are budget and sample design issues to consider in collecting data from multiple household members, but that diaries from multiple household members would be valuable in addressing important policy and behavior questions.

Data for International Comparisons

A key reason for conducting a time-use survey is to measure time use in nonmarket activities so that satellite accounts to the national income and product accounts can be produced. Household input and output tables similar to those produced by Landefeld and McCulla (1999) have now been produced in five other countries (Australia, Canada, Finland, Sweden, and Norway). No doubt, when the harmonized Eurostat time-use study is completed, more countries will produce these tables. In order to make comparable estimates of nonmarket household production across nations, and to make cross-country comparisons in time-use behaviors, it is important for the proposed U.S. time-use data collection to be as comparable as possible to other nations' studies. This need includes comparability in the classification of activities, for which there are several existing coding schemes for activities, including the United Nations International Trial Classification System for time use across different countries (see Horrigan et al. 1999 for a summary of the major classification schemes). With any standard that is implemented, special care will need to be taken to understand how question wording, examples used, and interviewer training differs across countries' surveys and how responses might reflect these differences. Despite the difficulties in standardizing data across countries, many workshop participants emphasized the value of time-use data for making cross-country comparisons and for informing policy.

FUTURE DATA COLLECTION AND
METHODOLOGICAL RESEARCH

No single survey will be able to collect all the data that can contribute to the policy questions that time-use data could address. For example, Katharine Abraham noted that the sample size proposed in the BLS survey will be too small to study the welfare population or those with disabilities. Also, to better understand household production, information on the technology available to the household and on the goods and services the household purchases would be needed. The CPS does not contain this information, and the BLS time-use survey will most likely not be able to collect it regularly because of scarce resources, although it may be possible to conduct a module to the CPS to collect such information or information on other specific topics.

Because no single time-use survey is going to be able to include all the information needed for policy-related research, to study specific populations (such as welfare recipients), or to study specific themes, time-use data could be collected as part of other surveys. Strategies would need to be developed for incorporating time-use studies and questions as part of existing survey programs or in new surveys targeted to the specific populations or topics of interest. For example, time-use questions and time diaries that parents filled out for their children were collected in 1997 as part of the Panel Study of Income Dynamics to better understand children's time use. Other potential examples mentioned at the workshop were to add a time-use diary to the Health and Retirement Survey for information on retirees and the elderly and to use the experiential sampling method to better understand time use in the workplace. New, targeted surveys of time use, like the California Activity Pattern Survey (described in Chapter 4) could also be developed. The feasibility of such studies will need to be further explored.

There are also several methodological considerations for time-use surveys that need further study, such as: designing stylized questions to obtain better estimates of time use in specific activities, assessing the quality of and exploring methods to improve recall on diary surveys and on stylized questions, using the experiential sampling method on a wider scale to collect time-use data, surveying multiple household members, and collecting diaries on multiple days for each sample member. In order to investigate some of the time-use topics of interest raised in Chapter 2, special methods may need to be considered and tested. For example, to study the time use of those with disabilities, questionnaire and time diary content considerations (perhaps asking if anyone helped the respondent with the activity) may need to be considered. As discussed above, a study that uses the experiential sampling method may be the most feasible way to collect data on time use in a market work setting. Workshop participants also stressed the importance of using developments in other diary surveys to improve time diary methods, for example, travel diaries, expense diaries, or food consumption diaries.

To further promote time-use surveys, many participants said that mechanisms for encouraging methodological research are needed. Time-use data can be applied to a broad range of social and economic behavioral and policy topics. Improving methods for collecting such data promises to be a rich area for research for the statistical community.

References

Almeida, D.
  1997 National Study of Daily Experiences: Examining Quantity and Quality of Child-Related Experiences Through Daily Telephone Diaries. Paper presented at the Time-Use, Nonmarket Work and Family Well-Being Conference, November 20.

Becker, G.S.
  1965 A theory of the allocation of time. *Economic Journal* 75(299):493-517.

Bittman, M.
  1999 An International Perspective to Collecting Time Use Data. Paper presented for CNSTAT Workshop on Measurement of and Research on Time Use, May 27-28, 1999.

Bryant, W.K., and C. D. Zick
  1996a An examination of parent-child shared time. *Journal of Marriage and the Family* 58:227-237.
  1996b Are we investing less in the next generation? Historical trends in time spent caring for children. *Journal of Family and Economic Issues* 17(3/4), 365-392.

Bryant, W.K., and Y. Wang
  1990 Time together, time apart: An analysis of wives' solitary and shared time with spouses. *Lifestyles* 11(1)(Spring):87-117.

Csikszentmihalyi, M., and I.S. Csikszentmihalyi, eds.
  1988 *Optimal Experience: Psychological Studies in Flow of Consciousness.* New York: Cambridge University Press.

Csikszentmihalyi, M., and R. Larson
  1992 Validity and reliability of the experience sampling method. Pp. 43-57 in De Vries, M.W., ed., *The Experience of Psychopathology: Investigating Mental Disorders in Their Natural Settings.* New York: Cambridge University Press.

(See Appendix B for summaries of papers presented at the workshop.)

Edin, K., and L. Lein
1997   *Making Ends Meet: How Single Mothers Survive Welfare and Low-Wage Work.*
        New York: Russell Sage Foundation.
Hamermesh, D.S.
1999   The timing of work over time. *The Economic Journal* 109(January):37-66.
Hill, M.S., A.R. Herzog, and F.T. Juster
1999   Time Use by and for Older Adults. Paper presented at the Workshop on Measure-
        ment of and Research on Time Use, May 27-28, 1999.
Hofferth, S.L.
1999   Family Reading to Young Children: Social Desirability and Cultural Biases in Re-
        porting. Paper presented at the Workshop on Measurement of and Research on
        Time Use, May 27-28.
Horrigan, M., D. Herz, M. Joyce, E. Robinson, J. Stewart, L. Stinson
1999   A Report on the Feasibility of Conducting a Time-Use Survey. Paper presented at
        the Workshop on Measurement of and Research on Time Use, May 27-28.
Huston, A.C., J.C. Wright, J. Marquis, S.B. Green
1997   How Young Children Spend Their Time: Television and Other Activities. Paper
        presented at the Time-Use, Nonmarket Work and Family Well-being Conference,
        November 20.
Ironmonger, D.
1997   National Accounts of Household Productive Activities. Paper presented at the Time-
        Use, Nonmarket Work and Family Well-being Conference, November 20.
Juster, F.T.
1985   Preferences for work and leisure. In *Time Goods and Well-Being.* F.T. Juster and F.P.
        Stafford, eds. Ann Arbor, MI: Survey Research Center, Institute for Social Research,
        University of Michigan.
1999   Time Use Data: Analytic Framework, Descriptive Findings, and Measurement Issues.
        Paper presented at the Workshop on Measurement of and Research on Time Use,
        May 27-28.
Juster, F.T., and F.P. Stafford
1985   *Time, Goods, and Well-Being.* Ann Arbor, MI: Survey Research Center, Institute for
        Social Research, University of Michigan.
Kalton, G.
1985   Sample Design Issues in Time Diary Studies. *In Time Goods and Well-Being,* F.T.
        Juster and F.P. Stafford, eds. Ann Arbor, MI:Survey Research Center, Institute for
        Social Research, University of Michigan.
Landefeld, J.S, and S.H. McCulla
1999   Accounting for Nonmarket Household Production within a National Accounts
        Framework. Paper presented at the Workshop on Measurement of and Research on
        Time Use, May 27-28.
Larson, R.
1989   Beeping children and adolescents: A method for studying time use and daily experi-
        ence. *Journal of Youth and Adolescence* 18(6):511-530.
Larson, R., and M.H. Richards
1994   *Divergent Realities: The Emotional Lives of Mothers, Fathers and Adolescents.* New
        York: Basic Books.
Michael, R.T.
1996   Money illusion: The importance of household time use in social policy making. *Jour-
        nal of Family and Economic Issues* 17 (3/4)(Winter):245-260

National Research Council
  1995   *Measuring Poverty: A New Approach.* Panel on Poverty and Family Assistance: Concepts, Information Needs, and Measurement Methods, C.F. Citro and R.T. Michael, eds. Committee on National Statistics, Commission on Behavioral and Social Sciences and Education: Washington, DC: National Academy Press.

Nordhaus, W.
  1999   Measurement of Time with Multiple Activities: Discussion Notes. Discussion presented at the Workshop on Measurement of and Research on Time Use, May 27-28.

Pollak, R.A.
  1999   Allocating Time. Paper presented at the Workshop on Measurement of and Research on Time Use, May 27-28.

Robinson, J.P.
  1985   The validity and reliability of diaries versus alternative time use measures. Pp. 33-62 in F.T. Juster and F.P. Stafford, eds., *Time Goods and Well-Being.* Ann Arbor, MI: Institute for Social Research, University of Michigan.
  1999   Methodological Features of the Time Diary Method. Paper presented at the Workshop on Measurement of and Research on Time Use, May 27-28.

Robinson, J.P., and G. Godbey
  1997   *Time for Life: The Surprising Ways Americans Use Their Time.* University Park, PA: The Pennsylvania State University Press.

Robinson, J.P., P. Switzer, and W. Ott
  1994   Microenvironmental Factors Related to Californians' Potential Exposure to Environmental Tobacco Smoke (ETS). Report Number 3 from the California Activity Pattern Survey. Environmental Protection Agency code number: EPA/600/R-94/116, August 1994.

Smeeding, T.
  1997   Time and Public Policy: Why Do We Care and What Instruments are Needed? Paper presented at the Time-Use, Nonmarket Work and Family Well-being Conference, November 20, 1997.

Szalai, A.
  1972   *The Use of Time: Daily Activities in Urban and Suburban Populations in 12 Countries.* The Hague, The Netherlands: Mouton.

U.S. Department of Agriculture
  1944   The Time Costs of Homemaking-A Study of 1,500 Rural and Urban Households. Bureau of Human Nutrition and Home Economics, Agricultural Research Administration, U.S. Department of Agriculture, Washington, DC.

U.S. Department of Labor
  2000   Budget Overview, Fiscal Year 2001. Washington, DC. Available: HtmlResAnchor www.dol.gov/dol/_sec/public/budget/budget01.htm [May 1, 2000].

Waite, L.J., and M. Nielsen
  1999   The Decision to Allocate Time Between Market and Nonmarket Activities. Paper presented at the Workshop on Measurement of and Research on Time Use, May 27-28.

Zuzanek, J.
  1999   Experience Sampling Method: Current and Potential Research Applications. Paper presented at the Workshop on Measurement of and Research on Time Use, May 27-28.

Appendixes

APPENDIX
A

Workshop Agenda

Workshop on Measurement of and Research on Time Use

National Academy of Sciences
Green Building, Room 104
2001 Wisconsin Avenue, NW
Washington, DC

May 27-28, 1999

Thursday, May 27, 1999

9:00 - 9:15   Welcome and Introductions
               Julie DaVanzo, RAND

9:15-12:00   Session 1: Research on Time Use: Setting the Context
               Chair: William Nordhaus, Yale University

9:15-10:00   Paper 1: Time Use Data: Analytic Framework, Descriptive
               Findings, and Measurement Issues
                   Author: F. Thomas Juster, University of Michigan

10:00-10:45   Paper 2: Notes on Theories of Time Use
                   Author: Robert Pollak, Washington University

10:45-11:00   Break

11:00-12:00   Session Discussion Time
                   Discussants:
                   Jack Triplett, Brookings Institution
                   Nancy Folbre, University of Massachusetts, Amherst

1:00-3:00   **Session 2: Determinants of Time Use: Applications of Time Use Data**
              Chair: Joseph Altonji, Northwestern University

1:00-1:35   Paper 1: The Decision to Allocate Time Between Market and Non-Market Activities
              Author: Linda Waite, University of Chicago
              Discussant: Joseph Altonji, Northwestern University

1:35-2:10   Paper 2: Family Reading to Young Children: Social Desirability and Cultural Biases in Reporting
              Author: Sandra Hofferth, Institute for Social Research, University of Michigan
              Discussant: Suzanne Bianchi, University of Maryland

2:10-2:45   Paper 3: Time Use by and for Older Adults
              Authors:
                 A. Regula Herzog, University of Michigan
                 Martha Hill, University of Michigan
                 J. Thomas Juster, University of Michigan
              Discussant: Daniel Hamermesh, University of Texas, Austin

2:45-3:00   Public Policy Implications
              Discussant: Rebecca Blank, Council of Economic Advisers

3:00-3:15   Break

3:15-3:50   **Session 3: Accounting for Nonmarketed Household Production Within a National Accounts Framework**
              Chair: Joseph Altonji, Northwestern University
              Authors:
                 J. Steven Landefeld, Bureau of Economic Analysis
                 Stephanie McCulla, Bureau of Economic Analysis
              Discussant: Dale Jorgenson, Harvard University

3:50-5:20   **Session 4: Conceptual Issues in Measuring Time Use— A Roundtable Discussion**
              Chair: Robert Michael, University of Chicago
              Participants:
                 William Nordhaus, Yale University
                 Jeanne Brooks-Gunn, Center for Young Children & Families, Columbia University
                 Francisco Samaniego, University of California, Davis

Roundtable Topics:
What aspects of time use are worth measuring?
Can the aspect of quality of time use be measured?
How can the problem of simultaneous activities be handled?
How can statistical models help address the 24 hour constraint and other time use survey issues?

Friday, May 28, 1999

9:00-11:30   **Session 5: Approaches to Measuring Time Use**
Chair: Norman Bradburn, National Opinion Research Center

9:00-9:30   Paper 1: Methodological Features of the Time Diary Method
Author: John Robinson, University of Maryland

9:30-10:00   Paper 2: Experience Sampling Method: Current and Potential Research Applications
Author: Jiri Zuzanek, University of Waterloo, Canada

10:00-10:15   Break

10:15-10:45   Paper 3: An International Perspective to Collecting Time Use Data
Author: Michael Bittman, University of New South Wales, Australia

10:45-11:30   Open Discussion Time
Moderator: Norman Bradburn, National Opinion Research Center
Discussant: Mihaly Csikszentmihalyi, University of Chicago

12:30-2:30   **Session 6: A Report on the Feasibility of Conducting a Time-Use Survey**
Chair: Francisco Samaniego, University of California, Davis
Author: BLS Time Use Survey Working Group
Michael Horrigan, Chair
Discussants:
Lorna Bailie, Statistics Canada
Nancy Folbre, University of Massachusetts, Amherst
Daniel Hamermesh, University of Texas, Austin

2:30-2:45   Break

2:45 - 3:45   Session 7: Where Do We Go from Here? —Roundtable
Discussion on Future Research Priorities
Chair: Julie DaVanzo, RAND
Participants:
Katharine Abraham, Bureau of Labor Statistics
Norman Bradburn, National Opinion Research Center
William Nordhaus, Yale University

4:00   Adjourn

APPENDIX
B

Summaries of Workshop Papers

TIME-USE DATA:
ANALYTIC FRAMEWORK, DESCRIPTIVE FINDINGS, AND MEASUREMENT ISSUES

F. Thomas Juster
University of Michigan

This paper provides an overview of time-use research. It starts with a brief description of an ambitious social accounting system that has time use as its core, moves to a description of important scientific and policy issues that can be examined with time-use data, explores differences among countries in two key areas of time-use research (labor/leisure choices and investments in children), examines alternative methods of measuring time use and concludes with a discussion of the optimum sample design for the collection of data on time use.

The unifying analytical framework of a time-use based social accounting system is the notion that the ultimate constraints on individual and societal change can be found in the availability of human time and the stock of wealth inherited from the past. Human time can be allocated to the market; to nonmarket production (cooking, cleaning, child care, etc.); to leisure activities (television viewing, socializing, etc.); or for biological maintenance functions (eating, sleeping, etc.). The outputs associated with these inputs of time are of various sorts: command over market goods and services is the output of time spent working for pay; nonmarket outputs such as orderly houses, well- or ill-behaved children, and gourmet meals are the outputs of nonmarket work in the household; improved health, skills, or stocks of information are additional nonmarket outputs; and direct enjoyments or satisfactions from the activities themselves are the final outputs of the system.

The role of capital stock in this view of the generation of well-being is crucial and has a rather unconventional flavor in comparison with the usual economic meaning of capital. Capital stock refers to a very broad range of settings that have the effect of conditioning the outcomes from the use of time in particular activities. This capital stock includes not only the effect of tangible assets such as factories, machinery, houses, cars, and other consumer durables, but also such tangible and intangible factors as human skills and knowledge, networks of personal associations, environmental assets like climate and water quality, sociopolitical assets such as the representational or the judicial systems, etc. In short, this framework regards capital stock as an appropriate term to describe a broad range of factors that condition the results of applying human time to various activities.

The paper highlights at least five distinct areas in which time-use data can make a substantial contribution to our understanding of the way in which economic and social systems function: (1) improving our understanding of the change over time in work and leisure activities and of the distribution of work and leisure between household members; (2) assessing the level of overall well-being; (3) understanding differences in economic systems characterized by different institutional arrangements; (4) examining a much broader definition of societal investments in the future, particularly investments devoted to the education and training of children; and (5) achieving a better understanding of distribution issues.

One of the most obvious benefits from the availability of time-use data is that it enables us to analyze a much more useful concept of work and leisure hours than the usual analysis of total available hours less paid work hours. Work hours as defined by a time-use study not only includes work for pay in the market, but also unpaid household work, commuting time to and from work, and work hours masquerading as leisure hours (shop talk over dinner) and leisure hours masquerading as work hours (long coffee breaks at work discussing fishing and golf).

The paper discusses methods for collecting time-use data and their strengths and limitations. The paper also discusses some sample design issues for time diary studies. It is ordinarily true that sample design issues are relatively straightforward and constitute the least problematic of survey design issues generally. But in the case of studies with time dairies, sample design issues are critically important and extremely complex. There is substantial room for disagreement about characteristics of an optimum sample design. The choices basically consist of the following:

• Select a random sample of households, select a random person within the household (in a multiperson household), and collect a single time diary from the randomly selected person within the randomly selected household on a randomly selected day of the year.
• Select a random sample of households, but in multiperson households, collect a time diary from all eligible persons in the household on a randomly selected day of the year.
• Select a random sample of households, collect time diaries from all eligible persons in that household, and collect multiple time diaries for each eligible person: an obvious choice for the number of diaries to be collected for each eligible person would be four—two weekdays, one Saturday, and one Sunday, spread randomly over the course of the year.

Which of these designs is most appealing depends in part on the analytic objectives of the study, but also on considerations of statistical noise, interclass correlation, and relative cost. The only systematic study of this topic concluded that the optimum design for maximizing the effective sample size for a given budget was a design that included two weekdays for each respondent, plus one Saturday and one Sunday, and also included spouses of respondents in married-couple households. In this analysis, no account is taken of any advantage accruing to analysis of microlevel data because the multiple observations per respondent design reduces the level of statistical noise in the time diary estimates. Thus, the conclusion that multiple observations per person are better than single observation from the perspective of minimizing sampling error is even more attractive if we take into account the reduction in statistical noise by collecting multiple diaries per respondent.

ALLOCATING TIME

Robert A. Pollak
Washington University, St. Louis

This paper provides a theoretical framework for estimating structural and behavioral relationships with time-use data. Four components of this framework are identified and discussed: technology, preferences, intrahousehold allocation and marriage market sorting. Starting with Becker's (1965) theory of household production, where households allocate their time (towards both market and nonmarket activities) to produce commodities that are then consumed and yield "utility," the paper describes these four components. Households use the technology available to them to produce the commodities. Individual preferences of household members also play a role in determining what a household produces, how the household spends its time producing, and how much is produced. The theoretical framework also covers how households allocate time towards producing commodities and how the commodities are allocated to household members. Finally, the paper describes a theoretical framework for how individuals sort into marriage (and form a multiperson household).

The paper also discusses implications of the joint production of commodities to the theoretical framework. An example of joint production is cooking a meal, which produces not only the meal, but also, if a person enjoys cooking, "process benefits" (intrinsic rewards, to use Juster's terminology). If so, then two goods are produced—the meal and the increase in satisfaction from spending time cooking the meal. This has implications for the theoretical assumptions of the production process.

Unlike the original theoretical framework laid out by Becker, this paper argues that households do not have preferences and utility functions, but that individuals within households have preferences and utility functions. The time allocated to household production and the benefits from household production are allocated within the household based on bargaining between household members and each member's preferences. The paper discusses the implications of this under different types of household preferences, such as interdependent preferences, when one household member's preferences are dependent on another household member's preferences, time use, and consumption, and preferences that differ across gender.

The paper also examines an application of the household production theory. The application discussed is how parental time spent with children translates into the production of a child's well-being and future well-being. The paper highlights the difficulty in empirically estimating this relationship, arguing that it is unlikely that a model could control for all determinants of the child's well-being (however measured) to estimate the relationship between the time parents spend with their children and the production of the child's well-being.

The paper briefly discusses how simultaneous activities (doing two things at once) should be treated in time-use studies. The paper proposes that activities be recorded as compound activities, so that time spent reading a book while flying in a plane is one category of activity (as opposed to two categories—reading and flying). As the paper points out, the problem with compounding activities is that the number of activities grow rapidly out of control. However, it is argued that a limited number of compounded activities that are particularly relevant for policy purposes could be accounted for in such manner on a survey. The example of being on call for child care duties (such as cooking while caring for a sleeping child) may be one such compounded activity.

THE DECISION TO ALLOCATE TIME BETWEEN MARKET AND NONMARKET ACTIVITIES

Linda J. Waite and Mark Nielsen
Center on Parents, Children and Work and
Alfred P. Sloan Working Families Center
University of Chicago

This paper examines the allocation of time by individuals and households between work in the market and nonmarket and household work. It traces labor force participation for men and women, married and single, over time. The paper also examines reasons for nonwork given by those who are not working and their reported sources of financial support. Joint labor force and nonmarket work statuses for married couples are also presented. In addition, the paper simulates husbands' nonmarket work activities in response to their wives working more hours and in response to working more hours themselves. Finally, the paper examines differences in lifetime market work decisions.

The paper begins with a summary of labor force participation rates for both men and women between 1962 and 1997. In this period, the percentage of men not in the labor force tripled, but remained modest (under 10 percent). However, labor force participation for women increased dramatically, from 42 percent in 1962 to 73 percent in 1997. The paper also describes the self-reported reasons for not working by those who were not working in the market. One noteworthy result is the increase in the number of nonemployed men who reported they are not working for pay in order to care for their family or home: in 1962, it was 1 percent; in 1997 it was 8 percent. For those who are out of the labor force, sources of support were also described. Of single women who are not working for pay, most reported that they received welfare or worker's compensation as a means of supporting themselves. Of single men who did not participate in the labor force, most reported receiving Social Security or worker's compensation as their means of support.

The paper also describes the number of hours that men and women devote to market and nonmarket work per week, using data from the National Survey of Families and Households. Women reported spending 18 hours per week (on average) in market work, while men reported spending 32 hours per week in market work. The average hours per week spent in nonmarket work is almost reversed by gender: women reported working 33 hours per week, and men reported working 18 hours per week.

The time that married couples spend in market and nonmarket work is also explored in the paper. A simulation is conducted of the responsiveness of husband's time spent doing five household chores (shopping, dishwashing, laundry, cooking, and cleaning) as the amount of time his wife spends working for pay increases. The simulation examines how the amount of time the husband spends in these five household chores varies as his wife's hours of time spent in the labor force go from zero to over 60 hours per week (holding the husband's time spent working for pay constant at the average for all men). Similarly, the responsiveness of husband's time spent doing household chores as his own time spent working for pay varies from zero to over 60 hours per week (holding constant the time his wife spends working for pay at the average for all women) is also simulated. Results of this simulation find that the amount of time husbands spend in nonmarket work changes less as the amount of time he spends working for pay varies, than when the amount of time his wife spends working for pay varies.

Finally, the paper discusses time spent in the labor market over a lifetime. The study finds that men over the age of 65 are working less now in comparison with the 1960s. The paper argues that further research on lifetime work decisions should be conducted.

FAMILY READING TO YOUNG CHILDREN:
SOCIAL DESIRABILITY AND CULTURAL BIASES IN REPORTING

Sandra Hofferth
University of Michigan

This paper compares measures of the time parents spend reading to their child gathered from single-item (stylized) questions and the time reported from time diaries filled out by the parents for the child. The importance of reading to young children in promoting language proficiency and literacy has been documented in many studies. Some data has also shown that children with more educated parents are read to more often than children with less educated parents. The paper further explores parental reports of reading to children, specifically, how reports gathered through single-item questions compare with those gathered through time diaries. The paper hypothesizes that parental reports of time spent reading to children is exaggerated through single-item questions relative to time diary reports. Furthermore, the paper hypothesizes that because more educated parents are likely to be more aware of the benefits of reading to their child, any social-desirability bias in reporting will be stronger for more educated parents. The paper also hypothesizes that there will be racial and ethnic differences in reports of time spent reading to children.

The paper uses data from the Child Development Supplement of the 1997 Panel Study of Income Dynamics (PSID). The supplement collected data on 2,394 children between the ages of 0 and 12, randomly selected from PSID respondents. The survey collected time diaries of the children's activities over a specified 24-hour period. The parent or caretaker of the child filled out the diary. One weekend day diary and one weekday diary was filled out for each child. The survey also used stylized questions on how often the parents read to the child: "How often do you read to (child)? Would you say never, several times a year, several times a month, about once a week, a few times a week, or every day?" The study compares responses to stylized questions on time spent reading to children with responses from time diaries on time spent reading to children.

Results show that 47 percent of children aged 3-5 were read to on a daily basis according to the stylized questions, but only 29 percent of the children were read to on a weekday or a weekend day according to the time diary reports. Holding the time diary as the standard, the paper concludes that parents exaggerate the number of times they read to their children on stylized questions. However, if reading reported through the diary on either a weekend day or a weekday is counted, 42 percent of children were read to, which is still under the amount reported from stylized measures.

The paper also regresses many demographic characteristics of the parents on an indicator for whether or not the parents reported reading to their child on a daily basis. This logistic regression includes a measure for whether or not the child was read to on a diary day as reported in the time diaries. The education level of the mother had a strong and positive association with reporting daily reading, which was given as evidence to support the hypothesis that more educated parents were more likely to exaggerate how often they read to their children.

TIME USE BY AND FOR OLDER ADULTS

Martha S. Hill, A. Regula Herzog, and F. Thomas Juster
Institute for Social Research
University of Michigan

This paper identifies key research issues concerning the time use of older adults and the time others spend caring for older adults. Key issues include: (1) how older adults spend their time, (2) how much time family members and relatives spend caring for older adults, (3) paid and unpaid work by older adults, (4) the activities of older adults and the impact of those activities on health, well-being, and mortality, and (5) the scheduling of activities of older adults. For each of these issues, the paper summarizes the implications for data collection. The paper also describes several existing data sets that have time-use data on older adults. They include time diary studies in the United States and elsewhere as well as longitudinal surveys containing time-use information.[1]

One of the key issues in time-use data collection for older adults is accounting for intergenerational transfers of time. Traditionally, research on intergenerational transfers of resources focuses on transfers of money and goods. However, there are also often transfers of care from the adult children to their dependent parents. Of policy interest is the degree to which labor market decisions are entwined with decisions to provide care for an older adult. Also of interest is the degree to which care from family members or resource sharing with family members (sharing housing, for example) substitutes for public assistance or for nonfamily private care providers. For researching these issues, extensive data are needed about different generations

---

[1]Data sets summarized are the 1965 Multi-national Time Budget Research Project, 1975-1976/1981-1982 Time Use Project, Americans Use of Time Project, Canadian General Social Surveys, Berlin Aging Study, Health and Retirement Study, Asset and Health Dynamics Among the Oldest Old, Panel Study of Income Dynamics, Americans' Changing Lives Survey, and Baltimore Longitudinal Study of Aging.

of extended families, including not only their time use, but also their sharing of other resources and their characteristics, needs and levels of resources.

Another issue relevant for time-use studies of older adults is the amount of time older adults spend in paid and unpaid work. Although many older adults are officially retired, they may still spend time working for pay. Older adults may also spend time in unpaid work, including household work. More broadly, it may also include time spent in volunteer activities and time spent caring for others. Older adults in good health often provide care for grand-children. They may also be the chief providers for a spouse in need of care. The authors argue that a combination of stylized questions and time diary data are needed to study the work of older adults. The potentially sporadic and irregular nature of this work means that time diaries tend to yield more accurate measures at the aggregate level while stylized questions asking about work over a typical day or week allow more accuracy at the individual level. The open format of a time diary reveals potentially unknown types of activi-ties; hence, stylized questions could be guided by time diary findings to focus on a wide range of work activities.

The paper also highlights the importance of understanding how the ac-tivities of older adults are associated with health, well-being, and mortality. The implication for data collection are that measures over time of both time use and well-being are needed. Time diaries are preferred over stylized diaries because they facilitate gathering contextual information on location and so-cial partners in activities, as well as avoiding having to pre-specify the type of activity.

Finally, the paper hypothesizes that older adults' schedules may be of both individual and public importance. Older adults usually have more flex-ibility in scheduling activities and so can take advantage of off-peak hours for such things as grocery shopping, use of roadways and public transport, and obtaining personal and household services. Older adults that are home dur-ing the day can also provide a sort of neighborhood watch. To explore these hypotheses, data are needed concerning the types and location of activities at different times of the day, on different days of the week, and in different seasons of the year.

In sum, the paper shows that the research issues regarding time use by and for older adults are diverse in their data needs. Some issues require stylized questions asking for typical amounts of time spent in pre-specified types of activities. Others require time diaries assessing not only the amount of time in activities but also social partners, location, and time of day. Some issues require data on all adults as well as older adults. Many require mea-sures in addition to time use; some require panel data. The authors stress that it is important to match the methodological approach to the research issue and to consider further methodological development.

ACCOUNTING FOR NONMARKETED HOUSEHOLD PRODUCTION WITHIN A NATIONAL ACCOUNTS FRAMEWORK

J. Steven Landefeld and Stephanie H. McCulla
Bureau of Economic Analysis

This paper describes how time-use data can be used to produce estimates that account for nonmarket household production in the national income and product accounts. The paper discusses the structural framework of satellite accounts and how nonmarket production fits into that framework. It then covers valuation issues for including household production in national accounts. Estimates of outputs and inputs of household production are given, and their impact on gross domestic product over time is also estimated. Finally, the paper offers some areas of further research and discusses the policy implications of the estimates.

The national income and product accounts (NIPAs) record the present value of the amount, composition, and distribution of income generated from market transactions in the U.S. economy. The accounts do not include for household production or unpaid housework, partly because of the difficulty in measuring and valuing nonmarket production. Satellite accounts offer a way to show measures of production that are not included in the standard set of national accounts while maintaining consistency with them. In the satellite accounts presented in this paper, estimates of household production were incorporated into measures of gross domestic product (GDP) from 1946 to 1997. Some of the resulting impacts on GDP are highlighted here.

The adjusted measures show a slower overall growth in GDP over the time period—7.1 percent annually instead of 7.3 percent annually—as the adjustments raise GDP by 43 percent in 1946 but by only 36 percent in 1997. The decreasing impact of the adjustments is a result of more women working in the labor force and spending less time working at home in 1997 than in 1946. Conversely, including consumer durables as investment raises GDP by 5 percent in 1946 and by 8 percent in 1997, reflecting the increased reliance on improved technology and household appliances as labor shifted from the home to the marketplace. Savings measures also increase, due to the reclassification of consumer durables; as a result, there is a slowdown in the fall of the personal savings rate, from 7 percent to 2 percent over the period. These and other results, taken together, suggest that the pecuniary tradeoffs between market production and home-based production have been positive and that recent concerns over falling savings and investment rates, especially in relation to other countries, may be exaggerated.

The paper also conducts an input/output analysis of the household for 1992. This analysis allows a more detailed look at the composition of household production. For instance, households, as reflected by personal consumption expenditures, have historically made up the largest portion of GDP. However, the expanded view in this paper reveals that households actually contribute more than just their final consumption. For instance, such expenditures on "cleaning, storage, and repair of clothing and shoes" is only $11 billion in 1992, while household laundry output is valued at $89 billion. The paper also reclassifies many household expenditures to illustrate that $2,596 billion (62 percent) of the conventional estimate for personal consumption expenditures of $4,209 billion in 1992 was actually spent on intermediate goods used in the household production process, and $471 billion was actually investment in consumer durables. In fact, only $524 (or 12 percent) of the conventional estimate of final consumption expenditures is actually final consumption.

METHODOLOGICAL FEATURES OF THE TIME DIARY METHOD

John P. Robinson
University of Maryland

This paper describes the diary method of collecting time use data. It describes the key features of the diary method, key uses of data collected from diaries, procedures to analyze time diary data, and the methodological properties of time diaries. Summaries of previous time diary studies and of alternatives to time diary studies are also given in the paper.

The paper argues that a key feature of the diary method of collecting time use information is that it acts like a "social microscope" into human behavior. The open-ended nature of a time diary allows respondents to describe in their own words what they were doing throughout the day. Diaries are typically collected for the entire day, so that the entire day's activities are accounted for, in contrast to other methods, such as stylized questions or experiential sampling studies, that do not collect information on the entire day. With time diaries, respondents are also able to designate what the most important activity was during a time frame if the respondent was simultaneously engaged in more than one activity. Although time diaries are often only collected for a single day, when they are accumulated across a large representative sample, aggregate accounts of how a population uses time can be estimated.

A limitation of time diary studies is that respondents report only what they want to report. As a result, some activities of a sensitive nature may not be reported accurately (e.g., sexual activity or reports of drug use). Recall error may also be an issue for time diary studies since respondents are typically asked to recall what they did one day ago. However, in comparison with time-use collected through single stylized questions (e.g., How much time each week do you spend cooking?), data collected through a time diary may be less prone to recall error.

The paper also describes reliability and validity features of the time diary method. Past studies of the reliability of time diary data are summarized. The paper concludes that time diary methods produce rather reliable accounts of time use at the aggregate level. The paper also summarizes validity studies of time-use data collected from time diaries. These studies have compared data collected from time diaries to data collected through a "random hour" technique (where respondents are contacted randomly throughout the day and asked to report what they were doing); through use of the "with whom" questions on the time diaries to cross-check spouses' reports of what they were doing at certain times; through the shadow technique, in which respondents are followed throughout a day and their activities cross-checked with self-reports of time use; and through direct observational studies, such as television camera monitoring studies. The results of these validity studies are reported in the paper.

Also summarized in the paper are procedures for analyzing time-use diary data. The usual way to analyze the data is to focus on the primary activity. However, time diary data have also been analyzed using the location of the activity, whom the respondent was with during the activity, the day of the week or the time of the day, and reported secondary activities.

EXPERIENCE SAMPLING METHOD: CURRENT AND POTENTIAL RESEARCH APPLICATIONS

Jiri Zuzanek
University of Waterloo

This paper gives an overview of the experience sampling method (ESM) of studying time use. The method monitors how respondents spend their time by using a pager, beeper, programmable wristwatch, or palm-top computer to randomly "beep" the respondent throughout the day. Once the respondent has been beeped, he or she records what he or she is doing at the time and records other items about the activity. This paper describes the method, compares its strengths and limitations to other methods of obtaining data on time use and highlights the potential applications of using it to study time pressure, psychological stress, and health.

The experience sampling method was developed mainly by psychologists interested in understanding behavior and states of consciousness throughout the day. As described above, the method randomly beeps individuals throughout the day, at which time, respondents, through a self-report form, answer a series of questions about what they were doing at the time. There are typically a core set of questions on the self-report forms, such as what the person was doing at the time, where he or she was, who he or she was with, and what were his or her thoughts at the time of the beep. Self-report forms usually include a series of questions about the experiential, emotional, cognitive, and motivational aspects of the activity the respondent is engaged in when beeped. Experience sampling studies have been used to measure qualitative aspects of daily life, to study leisure experiences, to study psychological and health disorders and behavioral and experiential correlates to them, and to study organizational behavior in the workplace.

The paper also discusses the general strengths and limitations of these studies in comparison with other methods for collecting time-use data, specifically, time diaries and stylized questions. One strength of the experience sampling method is that it can be used to study psychological states during activities throughout the day. In addition, there are no recall issues since respondents fill out the self-reports as soon as they are beeped. There is also likely to be less "normative editing" in these studies. The method can be used to study variations in psychological states across different activities, in different locations, with different individuals, etc. It can also be used to study human behavior in a natural context, as the respondents go about their daily lives, outside of a laboratory. Experience sampling studies can also be used to study interpersonal relationships, such as the "unmutual togetherness" that was described in the main body of this report. Finally, data collected through these studies can be analyzed as either a cross-section or as panel data, since multiple reports are collected from study respondents.

Limitations of experience sampling studies listed in the paper are that they can be intrusive, they may be subject to self-selection bias in who agrees to participate in the studies, they are not standardized, they do not completely cover the day (unlike time diaries, which cover the entire day), and they are more expensive than other methods.

The last section of the paper describes how these studies can be used to better understand the link between time pressure, stress, and health. The paper reports results of a preliminary analysis of experience sampling data that correlates respondent's daily moods and feelings of being pressured for time. Results show that being pressed for time (reported in a recall questionnaire) are negatively correlated with the respondent's sense of well-being as reported in the experience sampling method study, but positively correlated with reports of anxiety. The paper argues that such data can be used for further analyses of the dynamics of time pressure and emotional and behavioral conditions across weeks to understand uses of time and mental health.

AN INTERNATIONAL PERSPECTIVE TO COLLECTING
TIME-USE DATA

Michael Bittman
University of New South Wales

This paper summarizes some key theoretical and policy concerns for which time-use data can be used and discusses the implications for designing a time-use study. In doing so, the paper describes approaches used in time-use studies across different countries. The primary emphasis of the paper is that the best method for collecting time-use data depends on how the data will be used; the ultimate use of the data should be the guiding principle for choosing methodologies.

The paper describes two broad theoretical motives for collecting time-use data. The first is interest in conditions of economic progress. This includes changes in quality of life, social welfare considerations, and time spent caring for others. Quality of life is typically measured through national income accounts. However, national income measures count only goods and services produced and transacted through the market, not goods and services produced for a household's own consumption. This is especially important for measuring quality of life in less developed countries. Furthermore, national income accounts do not measure unpaid household work or transactions in the informal sector of the economy. The paper contends that distribution of free time in society should also be considered to better understanding social welfare. Finally, there are policy concerns to understanding time spent caring for others. The second theoretical motive for collecting time-use data is to better understand social changes. Specific social changes highlighted are changes in the organization of the household, in the division of labor within the household, and in the increased participation of women in the labor force.

These theoretical motives have implications for data collection. The first implication discussed in the paper is who should be sampled. The paper emphasizes that for informing welfare distributional questions, the household is the key sampling unit. The typical approach is to randomly select households and to collect time-use diaries from all household members. This method has been used in all three Australian time-use surveys and in the Eurostat pilot study. The age limits of sample selection are also relevant considerations. Most studies now do not have an upper age limit on sample members. Lower age limits are more common. The Eurostat pilot study collected diaries from those at least 11 years old. A 1989 Italian study collected time diaries for children aged 3 and older, and a Bulgarian study in 1988 had no lower age limit. (For younger children, diaries are filled out for the child by a care-giving adult.)

The theoretical motives also have implications for diary design. One design issue is the time span for which data are collected. Most studies collect data for a single day. The Australian study collected data for two days. Attempts have also been made to collect data for an entire week. Another issue is collecting information on secondary activities. If only primary activities are recorded, many activities of respondents will not be counted, especially those that tend to be "background" activities, for example, passive child care (being on call), listening to the radio, and conversation with others. In understanding care arrangements, the Eurostat pilot study asked not only who the respondent was with during the survey, but for whom an activity was conducted. The question was confusing, however, and coding costs increased. As a result, guidelines for the full Eurostat study do not call for inclusion of this question. Finally, the paper describes theoretical implications of designing questionnaires to be included with time diary studies. The paper suggests that to understand nonmarket work, it is important to collect information on household stocks of capital and on consumption of market services that may substitute for household labor. Also emphasized is the importance of collecting information on child care. A child care module was designed as part of Australia's last two national time-use studies.

APPENDIX
C
Proposed Coding System for Classifying Uses of Time for the Proposed BLS Survey

APPENDIX C Proposed Coding System for Classifying Uses of Time for the Proposed BLS Survey

Time Type	Major Group (1 digit codes)	2 Digit Codes	3 Digit Codes
Necessary Time	1. Personal care activities	11 Sleeping	111 Sleeping 112 Nap, rest
		12 Sleeplessness	121 Insomnia, sleeplessness, "toss/turn" in bed
		13 Personal hygiene and grooming	131 Showering, bathing, washing hands, brushing teeth 132 Going to the bathroom 133 Dressing or undressing 134 Shaving, putting on make-up, combing hair, etc. 139 Hygiene and grooming NEC
		14 Non-professional health care	141 Personal medical care (taking medication, vomiting, experiencing pain, exercise for medical conditions) 142 Rest because of illness, being in bed sick 143 Receiving (unpurchased) health treatments from non-professionals 149 Non-prof health care/treatments NEC

APPENDIX C   Continued

Time Type	Major Group (1 digit codes)	2 Digit Codes	3 Digit Codes
Necessary Time (*cont.*)		15 Eating/drinking	151 Eating a meal 152 Eating a snack 153 Drinking non-alcoholic beverages 159 Eating/drinking NEC
		16 Waiting related to personal care	161 Waiting to go to bed or fall asleep 163 Waiting to go to the bathroom or groom 164 Waiting for non-professional health care 165 Waiting to eat or drink
		17 Communication about personal care	171 Communication about personal care/self-maintenance
		18 Travel about personal personal care	181 Travel related to personal care/self-maintenance
		19 Personal care NEC	191 Respondent says 'personal', 'private', 'none of your business,' or reports sexual activity 199 Personal care/self-maintenance activities NEC
Contracted Time	2. Employment activities	21 Work for pay at main job(s)	211 Main job-usual hours-at work 212 Main job-extra hours-overtime 213 Main job-extra hours-work brought home 219 Main job NEC

22 Work for pay at other job(s)

    221 Other job-usual hours-at work
    222 Other job-extra hours-overtime
    223 Other job-extra hours-work brought home
    229 Other job NEC

23 Primary production and services for income not for establishments

    231 Unpaid work in family business or farm
    232 Preparing food or drink for sale
    233 Domestic home crafts or hobbies done for sale or exchange
    234 Building work done for income ("freelance work")
    235 Petty trading, street vending, collecting, scavenging items for sale (collecting aluminum cans, etc.)
    236 Providing services for income (child care, computing, cosmetic services, transport or delivery, etc.)

24 Work breaks

    241 Work breaks

25 Job search and related activity

    251 Looking at job listings
    252 Filling out applications or preparing resumes
    253 Interviewing for a job
    254 Applying for/collecting unemployment benefits/compensation
    255 Applying for/collecting welfare, food stamps or income subsidies
    259 Other job search activities NEC

APPENDIX C   Continued

Time Type	Major Group (1 digit codes)	2 Digit Codes	3 Digit Codes
Contracted Time (cont.)		26 Waiting/delays related to work or job search	261 Waiting or delay during work hours (fire drills, shut downs, waiting for appointments or meetings, etc.) 262 Waiting on-site for job interviews or to fill out forms for jobs, subsidies, compensation, etc.
		27 Communication about work or job search	271 Communication associated with but not part of work (calling in sick) 272 Communication associated with job interviews, subsidies, compensation, etc.
		28 Travel/commuting to/from work or job search	281 Travel in motion 286 Waiting for buses, trains, taxis, etc., related to work or job search
		29 Employment activities NEC	299 Employment or job search activities NEC
	3. Education activities	31 General education: school/ university	311 Attending class 312 Viewing education programs on TV for course credit

313 Unpaid student teaching; practicums
314 Special lectures outside the regular class time
315 Attending science or language labs

316 Registration activities or other administrative aspects of attending class
319 Other school related activities NEC

32 Job related training

321 Job related training, career education, professional conferences

33 Homework/study/research

331 Self study (not with computers), reading, etc.
332 Computing or assignment work done on computer
333 Group study
334 Working with tutors

36 Waiting related to education

361 Breaks at place of education
362 Waiting for class/training/tutorials to begin or resume

37 Communication about education

371 Communication about education

38 Travel related to education

381 Travel to classes, training, study groups

39 Educational activities NEC

399 Educational activities NEC

APPENDIX C Continued

Time Type	Major Group (1 digit codes)	2 Digit Codes	3 Digit Codes
Committed Time	4. Domestic activities	41 Food/drink preparation/cleanup	411 Food/drink preparation or service (include packing lunches, making meals or snacks, cooking for parties) 412 Preserving, freezing, drying food 413 Home brewing 414 Setting or clearing the table 415 Cleanup after food preparation or meals 419 Food and drink prep or cleanup NEC
		42 Laundry, care of textiles	421 Washing, loading, unloading washing machine 422 Hanging out or bringing in washing 423 Ironing 424 Sorting, folding textiles (clothes, linens, etc.) 425 Mending textiles, polishing shoes or other upkeep 426 Making clothes, knitting, sewing (not as hobby) 427 Sorting clothes for disposal; throwing out clothes 429 Laundry and textile care NEC
		43 Other housework	431 Interior cleaning of dwelling or related buildings 432 Exterior cleaning of dwelling or related buildings 439 Other housework NEC
		44 Grounds/animal care	441 Gardening 442 Yard or lawn care

443 Harvesting home production, hunting, fishing or
gathering food for household consumption
444 Grounds maintenance, garage cleaning, etc.
445 Pool care
446 Care for household pets
447 Care for livestock for household use only
449 Other grounds or animal care NEC

45 Home maintenance,
construction, and repair

451 Equipment repairs or maintenance
452 Dwelling construction or design
453 Interior maintenance or repair
454 Exterior maintenance or repair
455 Making furniture or other household goods
456 Making household furnishings
457 Heat/water/power maintenance, repair or provision
(include gathering, cutting, or stacking firewood)
458 Vehicle maintenance or repair
459 Home maintenance NEC

46 Household management

461 Paperwork, bills, tax returns, etc.
462 Budgeting money/time, organizing rosters/lists,
planning/organizing/decorating for family/household
events
463 Selling, donating, disposing of household assets
(including selling house or showing house for sale)
464 Recycling

APPENDIX C Continued

Time Type	Major Group (1 digit codes)	2 Digit Codes	3 Digit Codes
Committed Time (cont.)			465 Collecting, sorting, mail/parcels, checking messages and answering machines
			466 Packing/unpacking for a journey or move
			467 Putting away goods (groceries, etc.)
			468 Disposing of rubbish
			469 Other household management NEC
		47 Communication related to domestic act	471 Communication, discussion, "fights" about domestic activities
		48 Travel related to domestic act	481 Travel related to household work, maintenance, or management
		49 Domestic activity NEC	499 Domestic activity NEC
	5. Care for "dependent" household members (children, sick/disabled or elderly)	51 Physical or emotional care of "dependent" household members	

52 Teaching/helping/reprimanding "dependent" household members

53 Playing, reading, talking with "dependent" household members

54 Minding (supervising) dependent household members

511 Washing, dressing, feeding, grooming children
512 Medical/health care of children
513 Emotional care of children
514 Washing, dressing, feeding, grooming dependent household adults
515 Medical/health care of dependent household adults
516 Emotional care of dependent household adults

521 Teaching, helping, reprimanding, training children
522 Teaching, helping, reprimanding, training dependent household adults

531 Playing, reading, talking with children
532 Playing, reading, talking with dependent household adults

541 Supervision of children within the same room or play area
542 Supervision of children within the house, but not in the same room
543 "Passive" supervision of children not in the house (being 'on call')
544 Supervision of dependent household adults within the same room or play area

APPENDIX C Continued

Time Type	Major Group (1 digit codes)	2 Digit Codes	3 Digit Codes
Committed Time (cont.)			545 Supervision of dependent household adults within the house, but not in the same room
			546 "Passive" supervision of dependent household adults not in the house (being 'on call')
			549 Other supervision of dependent household members NEC
		55 Visiting care related establishments/schools	551 Accompanying a child to school, daycare, sports, lessons, etc.
			552 Accompanying a dependent household adult to school, sports, lessons, etc.
		56 Waiting associated with care of "dependent" household members	561 Waiting associated with care of children
			562 Waiting associated with "dependent" adult care
		57 Communication associated with care of "dependent" household members	571 Communication associated with care of children
			572 Communication associated with "dependent" adult care

58 Travel associated with care of "dependent" household members

581 Travel associated with care of children
582 Travel associated with "dependent" adult care

59 Care of "dependent" household members of NEC

598 Care of children NEC
599 Care of "dependent" adults NEC

6. Purchasing activities

61 Purchasing or returning goods

611 Purchasing/returning everyday consumer goods
612 Purchasing/returning durable household goods
613 Window shopping
619 Other purchasing of goods NEC

62 Purchasing service

621 Purchasing repair services
622 Purchasing/obtaining professional, government, administrative services
623 Purchasing personal care services
624 Purchasing medical or dental care services
625 Purchasing child or adult care services
626 Purchasing domestic/garden services
629 Other purchasing of service NEC

APPENDIX C Continued

Time Type	Major Group (1 digit codes)	2 Digit Codes	3 Digit Codes
Committed Time (cont.)		66 Waiting associated with purchases (5 minutes or more?)	661 Waiting at stores, shops, markets 662 Waiting in offices or for professional services 663 Waiting for maintenance, repair, or cleaning services 664 Waiting for personal care services 665 Waiting for medical or dental care 666 Waiting for deliveries of purchased goods 669 Waiting related to purchases NEC
		67 Communication associated with purchases	671 Scheduling appointments for service or purchases 672 Placing orders for goods or services by telephone, fax, or Internet 673 Discussing shipments, products, returned items 674 Other communication about purchases NEC
		68 Travel associated with purchases	681 Travel associated with purchases of goods or services
		69 Purchasing goods or services NEC	699 Purchasing goods or services NEC

7. Voluntary work and care

72 Unpaid helping/doing favors (for households)

- 721 Housework or cooking assistance
- 722 House maintenance or repair assistance
- 723 Babysitting
- 724 Care for disabled or ill adults
- 725 Correspondence assistance (letters, bills, forms)

73 Unpaid voluntary work (with organization)

- 731 Participating with an organization working directly with recipients
- 732 Participating with an organization not working directly with recipients

76 Waiting associated with voluntary work or care

- 761 Waiting related to help to other households
- 762 Waiting related to volunteering with an organization

77 Communication associated with voluntary work or care

- 771 Communication related to help to other households
- 772 Communication related to volunteering with an organization

78 Travel associated with voluntary work or care

APPENDIX C Continued

Time Type	Major Group (1 digit codes)	2 Digit Codes	3 Digit Codes
Committed Time (*cont.*)			781 Travel related to help to other households
			782 Travel related to volunteering with an organization
		79 Voluntary work or care NEC	
			798 Help to other households NEC
			799 Voluntary work with organizations NEC
Free Time	8. Social and community interaction		
		81 Socializing	
			811 Talking, chatting, social conversation
			812 Celebrating, having parties with friends or family
			813 Eating, drinking with non household members in own home
			814 Eating, drinking with non household members or household members in public place
			819 Other socializing NEC
		82 Entertainment	
			821 Attending musical performances, concerts, symphonies
			822 Attending plays, ballet, opera
			823 Attending cinema, art films, drive-in movies
			824 Attending fairs, circuses, parades, amusement parks, ice follies, fireworks
			825 Visiting zoos, botanical gardens, planetariums, observatories

826 Visiting museums, art galleries, exhibitions, libraries
827 Visiting historical or archeological sites, etc.
828 Visiting casinos, bingo halls, arcades
829 Entertainment NEC

83 Attendance at sports events

831 Attendance at professional or amateur sporting events
832 Attendance at professional or amateur racing events
839 Attendance at sports events NEC

84 Religious/ritual activities

841 Personal religious practice (meditation, prayer, etc.)
842 Religious ceremonies, rituals
843 Planning, practicing, rehearsing, decorating, preparing for religious ceremonies, celebrations, rituals
844 Socializing associated with religious ceremonies/ rituals
845 Cleaning up after religious ceremonies, celebrations, and rituals
849 Religious activities NEC

85 Community participation

851 Attending meetings
852 Civic ceremonies or celebrations (civil weddings, ribbon cuttings, parades, inaugurations)
853 Planning, practicing, rehearsing, decorating, preparing for civic ceremonies and celebrations
854 Socializing associated with civic ceremonies or celebrations
855 Cleaning up after civic ceremonies, celebrations
856 Civic obligations (jury duty)

APPENDIX C   Continued

Time Type	Major Group (1 digit codes)	2 Digit Codes	3 Digit Codes
Free Tme *(cont.)*			857 Answering surveys, polls, and censuses
			859 Community participation NEC
		86 Waiting related to social and community interaction	861 Waiting for social or community interaction to begin
		87 Communication related to social and community interaction	871 Communication about social or community interaction (checking on time, preparations, etc.)
		88 Travel related to social and community interaction	881 Travel associated with social or community interaction
		89 Social and community interaction NEC	899 Social and community interaction NEC
	9. Recreation and leisure	91 Sport and outdoor activity	911 Walking, hiking, jogging, and running
			912 Biking, cycling, skiing, skating, skate or snow boarding, horseback riding

913 Ball games
914 Gymnastics, aerobics, work-outs, marital arts, wrestling, yoga, ballet, or other dance
915 Swimming, water gymnastics, and water skiing
916 Boating, sailing, canoeing, and rafting
917 Gliding, balloning, and flying
918 Camping, hunting, fishing for sport
919 Other sport or exercise NEC

92 Games, hobbies, art, and crafts

921 Card, paper, board, parlor games/crosswords
922 Computer games or computing as hobby
923 Hobbies, collections, albums, etc.
924 Handiwork and crafts (sewing, knitting, weaving)
925 Visual or graphic arts
926 Performing arts/music
929 Games, hobbies, arts, crafts NEC

93 Reading/writing

931 Reading book, magazine, and newspaper
932 Reading CD rom
933 Being read to (in-person or books-on-tape)
934 Writing for leisure/pleasure (letters, poetry, diaries, cards, books, short stories, etc.)
939 Reading/writing NEC

94 Audio/visual media

941 TV watching/listening
942 Video Watching
943 Listening to radio

APPENDIX C Continued

Time Type	Major Group (1 digit codes)	2 Digit Codes	3 Digit Codes
Free Time (cont.)			944 Listening to records/tapes/CDs (other than books)
			945 Accessing Internet
			949 Other media use NEC
		95 Attendance at courses (except school or university)	951 Attendance at personal development courses
			952 Attendance at art/craft/hobby courses
			959 Attendance at courses (ex. school/university) NEC
		96 Other free time	961 Relaxing, resting
			962 Doing nothing
			963 Thinking
			964 Worrying
			965 Drinking alcohol/social drinking
			966 Smoking
			967 Looking at memorabilia
			968 Teasing, joking around, messing around, laughing, pestering
			969 Other free time NEC
		97 Communication associated with free time	971 Communicating about free time

98 Travel associated with
    free time

        981 Recreational driving/riding for pleasure
        982 Holiday travel
        989 Other travel associated with free time NEC

99 Leisure and recreation NEC

        999 Leisure and recreation NEC

0. No activity

  00 No activity

        001 Time gap with no reported activity
        002 Uncodeable activity

SOURCE: Horrigan et al. (1999).

APPENDIX
D
Draft Questionnaire for Proposed BLS Survey

APPENDIX D   Draft Questionnaire for Proposed BLS Survey

Survey Script		Explanatory Notes
Element 1: Updating CPS Data	↑	Because time use can vary in important ways depending on the respondent's labor force status and the composition of the respondent's household, it is important to have up-to-date information on household characteristics. The first portion of the survey will include an update of selected CPS questions, using a "dependent interviewing" approach.
Element 2: Other Background	↑	Additional background data that would improve time use analyses, such as data on home ownership, could be collected either as a standard part of the survey or as a periodic addition.
Element 3: Time-Use Component	↑	This will be the typical BLS telephone survey introduction. This version was used in the pilot test during the summer of 1997.
Introduction		
"This study is sponsored by the Department of Labor, Bureau of Labor Statistics. I'd like to ask you some questions about how you spent your time **yesterday**.		

APPENDIX D   Draft Questionnaire for Proposed BLS Survey

Survey Script	Explanatory Notes
Your participation is completely voluntary. The Bureau of Labor Statistics will use the information that you provide for statistical purposes only and will hold the information in confidence to the full extent permitted by law. This interview usually takes about 25 minutes. The best way to collect accurate information on the way people use their time is to complete a diary listing of all their activities over a 24-hour period. We start our diary at midnight (reporting day)." *Example for respondent* Let me give you an example: At midnight I was asleep until 7:00 a.m. (reporting day) morning. I took a shower and got dressed between 7:00 and 8:30. I made breakfast for my family between 8:30 and 9:00. We all ate breakfast together until 9:30. I cleaned up the dishes after breakfast until 9:45. After that I read the newspaper and I	 Since the time-use survey is a semi-structured interview, dependent upon the respondent verbatim accounts of their day, it is necessary for the interviewer to provide the respondent with a brief example of how to proceed. This version was used during our pilot test. The key elements are: a. clarification of the correct reporting day (shown

watched television until 10:30. Then I drove with my daughter to the mall from 10:30 to 10:50. We were shopping for clothes until 1:00.

Time-use reports

Now I would like to find out how you spent your time from midnight (reporting day) until midnight last night. If we get to times you spent working at a job, just tell what time you started working and what time you stopped.

↑

my linking it with the wake-up time of the reporting day).

b. indications of how to proceed sequentially (shown by reporting several tasks in an orderly temporal progression), and

c. training in the level of detail that is required from the respondent (shown by omitting specific details about the grooming process and by including activities such as travel, as well as the location and key persons included in the activity.

Following the conventions used by other time-use surveys, we are not asking for the same level of detail for work times as for non-work times. Since the vast majority of work times are simply spent in a series of "work" activities, researchers have generally chosen to save interview time by giving the general "work" classification to that entire time period. Since non-work time is more multi-faceted, it is necessary for respondents to itemize

APPENDIX D Draft Questionnaire for Proposed BLS Survey

Survey Script	Explanatory Notes
	each activity in more detail in order to correctly classify them. We propose, however, going beyond the traditional approach by asking respondents if they stopped working at any time in order to do something that was unrelated to their work. This should enable us to collect personal, social or non-marked work activities that have been omitted and, consequently, underestimated in the past.
Initial activity At midnight (reporting day) morning, what were you doing?	→ Interviewer will type the verbatim response here. This is coded for analysis as an "initial" or "primary" activity.
Start time What time did this start?	→ Interviewer will enter the starting time.
Stop time What time did this end?	→ Interviewer will enter the ending time.

↑ Following the Canadian procedure, interviewers would be asked to classify the response into categories similar to these:

Location
Where were you?/were you still ...
(accept only one answer)

PLACE

a. respondent's home
b. work place
c. someone else's home
d. other place (type-in verbatim location)

OR IN TRANSIT

e. car (driver)
f. car (passenger)
g. walking
h. bus or subway (include street cars, commuter trains or other public transit)
i. bicycle
j. other such as airplane, train, motorcycle (type-in verbatim location)